1

Elton D. Jones

2011

Publishied 2023

Published by: Jones Publishing LLC

Text Design by: Elton D. Jones

Cover Design by: Elizabeth E. Rios-Jones

A CIP record for this book is available from the Library of
Congress Cataloging-in-Publication Data

ISBN-13: 978-0-9836783-4-2

Distributed by:

Ingram Content Group
1 Ingram Blvd
La Vergne, TN, 37086
Printed and bound in Location by Lightning Source Inc.

Elton D. Jones

2011

Dedication

Keep Striving
During Times of Hardship
No Matter What the Obstacles

Your mind believes what you tell it, so tell it positive things.

Mastering Law of Attraction

10

Don't ever think people don't like what you do. They just don't like the fact that you're the one doing it. Either way....KEEP GRINDING

26

Nipsey Hustle

Part of being authentic is actively living your purpose. Surround yourself with people who encourage you to be who you were meant to be.

44

Mastering Law Of Attraction

If they not giving you energy putting a battery in your back let them go! Friends/family/relationship or business! No fear.

62

Meek Mill

Be your own biggest fan, your own biggest believer, and put it on your back and carry that weight.

80

Nipsey Hustle

Every morning is a fresh beginning everyday is the world made new. Today is a new day.

I love when they think you are nobody and you turn out to be the GOAT.

99

Eminem

Let everything you do be done in love.

Corinthians 16:14

116

A positive attitude causes a chain reaction of positive thoughts, events, and outcomes. It is a catalyst and it sparks extraordinary results.

134

Mastering Law of Attraction

You have to have confidence in your vision or else no one else will trust in it.

152

Mary Katrantzou

When we face the worst that can happen in any situation, we grow. When circumstances are at their worst we can find our best.

171

Elisabeth Kubler-Ross

One day, if you have a little bit of talent and a lot of hard work, you're going to find out who you are.

189

Massimo Bottura

Don't try to figure out what other people want to hear from you; figure out what you have to say.

206

Barbara Kingsolver

Our doubts are traitors, and make us lose the good we oft might win, by fearing to attempt.

225

William Shakespeare

Optimism is a perfectly legitimate response to failure.

Stephen King

242

I will either find a way, or make one.

Hannibal

259

That is happiness; to be dissolved into something complete and great.

276

Willa Cather

Remember that not getting what you want is sometimes a wonderful stroke of luck.

289

Dalai Lama

And it shall come to pass afterward that I will pour out my spirit on all flesh; your sons and your daughters shall prophecy, your old men shall dream dreams , your young men shall see visions, and also on my menservants and on my maid servants I will pour out my spirit in those days.

Joel 2:28-29

The older women likewise, that they be reverent in behavior, not slanderers, not given to much wine, teachers of good things-
Titus 2:3

Your mind believes what you tell it, so tell it positive things.
Mastering Law of Attraction

It Aint Over

You may have won this battle,
With all hopes that I would fight no more.
My Lord's is the biggest battle
That was lost in the physical,
But victorious in the spiritual world.
My God always has a plan
So know that this aint over.
This war is to be much bigger than that;
To still have faith,
Through all that you may have stolen:
Wife; Kids; and Career!
Thanks to my God She made you spare my life.
Now we create one more testament for goodness
While rebuilding this broken down rite.
Torn down to the weakest point,
But never to the point of giving up.
It is when we are the weakest
That God is the strongest within us.
You meant for this to hurt me,
But by my God it will be used for good!
In Earth as it is in Heaven;
Even in your world my God rules.
Knowing this war is much bigger than me
I pray to fill my space with your son!
This war started in Heaven
Then from hell to this Paradise we've cum.
Well it aint over!
Till this war is completely One
Never giving up!
Patiently waiting till the day,
When again will rise the morning Son.

Thank You God

Through all that we've been through;
These last 12 years have been harsh.
Thank you God!
Through this storm; You've brought us out.
So much of this has been allowed!
How many did not make it here?
Took life!
And to this point!
You have brought me to the release date in this.
Through it all dear Lord,
Thank you for saving a wretch like me.

Thank you God for the strength,
Just to hold on a little bit longer through gritted teeth.
Made it through so many storms
And in the midst of each one,
Never coulda seen how we coulda made it.
Looked back to the reason,
And only the foundation was still left done

Built this house upon Christ,
Or there would have been nothing left.

Thank you God for this fellowship!
Such a relationship to be in your rest.
Thank you God that through it all
You have still brought us only your best.

The King Is Here!

Thank you for your holy spirit
I can feel your presence in me!
You are always here
Even when we can't feel you physically near to me.
Knowing that when I can't walk
Then it is that you carry me.
Found me crying down on my knees,
And you still wouldn't let the world bury me.
Just picked me up!
When I only wanted to stay down on the ground.
When the world continued to kick!
Suggesting for me to just stay down on the ground.
It was the whisper in my ear
Of your ever present voice
Advising me to keep on living, and to not give up;
Continue to push forth!
Reminding me to stand tough!
Put myself aside
And only think upon your mind
No matter what this world may try.
This world is not of God's will.
Heavenly and Holy:

I continue to read your scriptures.
Eyes battered and bruised,
Yet I continued to keep reading the scriptures.
Lips bleeding and swolen,
still reading through loose tooth.
Yet I continue to chant your name.
Talking to myself repeating,
"Just to get out of the way."
Let the Lord do IT'S work
In IT'S own way.

All things are possible for you
Please take this cup of suffering away.....
This is one of my favorites,
Hope that you can finish that phrase.

Just to be close to the King
Sometimes is to be so far away.
My earthly father wasn't always around
Yet I still turned out O.K.
An anomolie to the stereotypes
From trouble I turned away.
My city still demanded me back.
When from it,

I ran away.

Landed in a bad situation;
Got me down on bended knee.
Watching as my world fell away;
Caved in all around me.
When it is that I am weak,
The King Is strongest within.
Giving my all away
Knowing that She lives within.

No I won't even cry,
This is not about selfish gain
Whatever it is that our Father tells me to do
My only reply is O.K.
Faith over fear!
No way will He let you hide the way.
In here to do some fishing, and I cant do that locked away.
The biggest demons are the best ones;
Only moved by prayer and fasting
I am a prisoner of Jesus Christ.
satan stand behind me.

Prisoner of Jesus Christ

I am a prisoner of Jesus Christ
And my cell number is G-O-D.
This negative will be moved to positive
As long as it's the Lord who moves before me.
Aligning my path,
When I thought that there was no more road to go.
Please continue to speak through me
Allowing these people to see the correct way to grow.
My brothers keeper!
So I find myself in hell with him.
Looking to bring satan back from here,
But I know that only a few will dare leave from him.
Many prefer to be blind, and deaf,
So that they can continue being dumb.
Using that as an excuse, for when my Jesus cums.
Many will reach into the pit,
But how many will gladly dive in?
Knowing that we can't be touched
However could you believe that you could win?
When even here, our Father is.
Leaving His light in order for us to move
Even by darkness, Her light will continually illuminate this!
Daring to change the world!
Even when in the face of evil we remain.
Who will try to save the world,
Starting with each individual soul that you can take?
How many will you bring?
Hands to the soul of Christ?
Because conversions will cover sin
I know that I have points in the right.
In here to be a beacon,
Take some back to the mind of Christ.

Do Not Get Discouraged 05-14-11

When life doesn't go as we planned it,
And the flesh wants to just pass away
We must remember that this warfare is spiritual.
We battle on for yet another day!
Even Christ's walk wasn't made easy
And He still walked with God till the last day!
Never giving up on our Father
Though many curveballs were thrown his way.
To sit at the left and right of the King!
What is it that we must be willing to give away?
I know that your story may be bad,
But consider the story of the person
Sitting to the left and right of your space!
Continue to meditate and pray.
satan gets no seat in here, unless it's you he comes through.
he must flee from here! All according to our faith.
From the Lord,
Job never turned away.
So why would I harden the heart,
Knowing that God still lives in you today?
His love continues to pump through this heart.
Behind these bars for three or for thirty three years and still
satan you can't change this heart through all you put me through.
These years are only time spent with my Lord
Consecrated! Getting to better know you.
Take away my bible and Christian relics,
But there's one thing that you must know.
This word is embedded in my heart,
And there you cannot go!
Do not get discouraged!

My saints continue on by faith
I am Paul! Or call me Peter,
Because I refuse to lose this faith!
Sending word to Fearless Faith
Knowing that it will help the people!
God sends me these words.
So I have faith that my paper bag letter
Will well receive you!

Just To Face Today 05-15-11

How do I face today?
Knowing that yesterday aint yet gone.
Remnants of the tattered past,
Still tagging right along!
Far and near, the Lord has forgiven,
What the world still holds overhead.
If it wasn't for the faith in my Lord
I would have been went to bed;
To a perpetual sleep.
Forced to face the past no more.
This world hopes that we will circle;
Get trapped in a revolving door.
The defintion of insanity;
Doing the same thing with hopes of a different result.
To change the people, places,
And habits is the only way out!
Until we're forced into a spin-off;
A dizzying exchange!
How can I still make a difference?
Though physically, I find myself stored away!
Stripped of life twice!
Now you want to take it again.
I'll dance for God out here naked
Mind only set on praising him!
To forgive and forget,
Or to hold a long term grudge?
Even when we can no longer even remember what for.
If God doesn't believe in revenge!
SHE will avenge for what's been stolen
Thank Him everyday
Even when our good deeds go bad
Yes even Jesus went to prison!

Having all faith in his Dad!
Never said a mumbling word;
Why has thou forsaken me?
Only you have the power oh Lord.
Yet you don't save me from mine own enemies!
Him who the Lord chastens, is
To be ready for a wonderful change.
See the silver lining in those dark clouds?
The rainbows just beyond that dark rain!
You see the dove still following?
Though we may currently reside in such a horrible place.
We have to muster up the courage to fight!
For just one more day.
The future ain't promised,
And next week is too far away
But today I can make a difference
By simply standing on this faith.
Is there anything too hard for the Lord?
In the mount of the Lord it is provided
How can we ask for the strength of Joseph,
But not be willing to go his way?
There's only one way to our Father's house
And that's through that narrow gate.
Israel we can't turn back now!
There is no other way.
My tomorrow may be overwhelming,
For yesterday this only I pray,
Grant me the strength oh Lord,
Just to face today.

My Light Shines Bright 05-16-11

Yeah this is a dark place,
But even in here She shines bright.
This holy glow emitted by He, who knows no darkness of night!
Whole mind set on doing right!
Through it all I've learned to trust in Jesus.
To God be my witness,
It was me that got me into this.
Watch as my jailors bow down!
I'll invite them back up,
And then allow them to lock me down.
When like Hancok I could rise up.
Not afraid of this darkness!
Fearless to be my faith.
Thank you Pastor Cotton
For continuing to lead us in the correct way.
God is divine, and He does great works through you!
All my love be to the congregation
I know that we will pull through.
Sister Ross you walk in health.
Brother Fred 100% is what you give.
Much love to the Tripletts.
Mom we will again see brighter days after this!
Minister Briscoe you are an angel.
Mother Linda, keep on praying.
Your petitions have been heard in heaven,
But the reply is to come later.
Shots out to my ole wise men:
Reverend; and brother Howell!
Keep elevating the space
I'll always speak to mother Howell.

Just Beyond That Darkness 05-16-11

The silver and gold lining, stitched right into those dark clouds.
Eagles flying freely overhead,
I watch as the birds fly in and out.
Coming in daily to eat this bread;
My Lord is a miracle worker.
When we just sit down and count the blessings,
It's all about what we put in the ground.
The seed that we sow:
Positive or negative?
Not having enough, or to only focus on the blessings.
We made it through just one more day
Although I know yesterday may have been rough.
How could I ever be depressed?
Or hanging my head down low?
When my father gives the Holy Spirit to each of us
How low did Jesus have to go?
The battle is already won.
What part of that do you not yet know?
satan's attempts to deceive are weak
When we are familiar with what God already knows.
Just keep reading the book,
But apply the principles all throughout our world.
Everytime a door closes,
Just have faith and hold out your hands!
How could we curse Jesus, because things don't go as we planned.
The heavenly Father is always right on time;
Who else could raise Lazarus from the dead?
The material is not important,
Just a resource of the world, all about the heavenly currency
Which remains to be the word!
His word will never change
But gold and silver will pass away.

What if today was deemed the end?
Would you be one of the many who would have to stay?
Just beyond that darkness
But only according to Your level of faith!
Can you hear my chains ringing?
As I continue to praise the Lord each and every day
These bars keep slamming shut,
But I only see open doors
Call me something special
I know I'm one of a kind,
Will never give up on my Lord
Only continue to fight!
When the world says we aint good enough
Only know that Jesus died
And when naysayers said it couldn't be done.

Born To Be a Soldier 5-17-11

Look at me on this battlefield,
Fighting in the name of the Lord
My environment, my country,
Not even the State Police can hold me captive any more.
This is all Training,
Getting ready for the army of my Lord.
Knowing that it's specific things that He needs me to learn.
I travel through hades, on a quest to know more.
Not saying She put me here,
It's my own choices that took me from Her.
No matter where I may make my bed,
His love is what keeps me warm.
Showering me with innate goodness
When you could have just washed me away in one of those storms.
Still giving me a second chance!
When the world say's it is time for me to be gone.
No matter how heavy the gravity may get
We must never give up on faith!
Just continue to enjoy the journey
Knowing the intended destination is His way
My lord is the ruler of all
No matter how dark the storm we may have to face.
Knowing that it is not over,
Until I physically decide to fade away.
Sampson continued to fight, even after he decided to give up;
Giving the loved enemy the secret,
The way to relieve his powered up.
My Lord hung for many days,
Yet he prayed right up into the last hour.
His strength is made perfect in weakness
To Him I give all the power.
Though we walk through the valley of death
We must always stand up.

Don't ever think people don't like what you do. They just don't like the fact that you're the one doing it. Either way....KEEP GRINDING

Nipsey Hustle

Head In The Clouds 5-18-11

See my mindset on freedom, while my body is trapped in here
My soul you can never take
No matter how long you keep my body in here.
Some talk about selling the soul
As a ticket to get free.
This soul is only the lords, even if the release date was set for the
Year 2116.
You see my head is in the clouds,
Mind set on heaven.
No one said it would be easy
Just because my birth number is four sevens.
Only those who know me, will truly understand;
7 pounds, 7ounces, 7th month and 7th date.
Tell me I ain't a part of God's plans.
satan step out of the way
You can call me the messenger,
Here to deliver word for my Lord,
But how many of the people will listen?
Many will just ignore.
Figuring this spiritual battle ain't real;
Jesus was also a messenger,
Speaking truth to his disciples,
Yet they couldn't understand the meanings,
Or decipher such heavenly messages.
These physical problems aint real!
Once we receive the heavenly message.
We dance in the rain for our Lord
A small way to thank Him
For all of His big blessings.

Constant prayer and continual praise
I will serve the Lord until here I serve my last day.
No I aint perfect, made atonement for me going astray.
Believe the words of Jesus
So evil can't trick me into again going any other way.
I fly high with eagles,
Or lay low with the doves
Jesus is our spiritual leader
So how much time will you devote to love?

To Remain Faithful

When life grabs a hold of you, and makes you trip and fall
Skinning up your face, bruising your knees, making you want to
Just bawl.
When loved ones are taken away, and we're left wondering where
Did they go?
When that homeless person is running the street, playing guitar
Out in the cold.
With the young ones sent to war, and the economy doing bad
Separated from our true love, and the heart remains sad.
When bad forces just seem to keep winning, no matter how
Much they may be sinning.
When we come down with sicknesses, where is it that we are to
Go in order to get the healing?
If we quarrel with family members, who wins and who loses?
Earthquakes and natural disasters!
What are we even doing in here?
God give me confirmation; Tell me to build another boat.
Fire and brimstone! Why are you taking so long?
This life is not worth living. Hurry up and get this all done!
When life becomes overwhelming,
Why do we keep the faith in your begotten son?
We're too tired to move on, how do we finish the race?
Why fight the good fight? When Jesus already saved the day
Physically free of this wicked place.
Why does my heart keep on hearing this; God sending these songs.
Led by the Holy Spirit, then why can't I see it?
Hearing Her when She calls, but why do I believe in it?
When I fall off of this cliff, who embraces the harness?
When I fall off of this cliff, why do I try and climb it again?
What's the reason for believing, this soul can still win?
What's the reason to keep believing, He sent his only son?
How long oh Lord, before you avenge this blood?
How long oh Lord, before his time is done?

This Isn't Even About Me 5-22-11

Find me spending time in Hades
To become the messenger of peace!
I'll do anything if called by my Lord,
This time is not even about me.
Jesus had to give it all
In order to cum and save.
Given as a sacrifice, in this sinful place
When He was already a King, here to help us go the right way.
Never said a mumbling word!
Just continued on by faith.
Though His attackers kept spitting on him
The Lord's word is all that he would say.
Quoting the scriptures,
Knowing God's will must be the next play,
Maybe tomorrow! Since I refuse to die today.
My Lord now sits back in the kingdom,
Now that She has opened the way.
"I am the way, the truth, and the life. No one comes to the
Father unless he comes through the son."
When the mother asks,
"What must my son's do to sit at the left and right of the King?"
"Can You drink from my cup? This here cup of suffering"
We must go through it!
In this so corrupted life,
But the whole time we are told, to praise the name of Jesus Christ.
This aint about you
All of the suffering you must go through.
It's simply for someone following,
Generations moving forward from behind you!
Keep the mind set on Jesus
Knowing that He has opened the gates.
Yes it looks impossible,
But we must follow through the narrow way.

Model Citizen 5-22-11

"You have done all of this wickedness, Yet do not turn aside from following the Lord, but serve the Lord with all your heart."
1 Samuel 12:20

Show me a perfect person,
And I'll prove to you a beautiful liar.
My lord choose his disciples,
And for each one He knew exactly why
What they were destined for.
God summoned a few, and none of those were perfect;
They all had work that He needed them to do,
Although they all were broken.
Lost and confused,
You can make all the excuses in the world, God will only make a
Way around em.
What would we do without the tender mercies of Her?
I'm a sinner and I just need to be grounded.
Thank God for sending Jesus to forgive us.
Even a new chance for those locked away and bounded!
Will live on for another day, just to tell the tale
Screaming out my Jesus name, echoing from cell to cell.
"If we confess our sins, She is faithful and just to forgive us our sins
And to cleanse us from all unrighteousness."
We can only make it to tomorrow, because of what He does Today.
Just because we are forgiven,
Does that mean we are to go deeper into the wrong way?
Why certainly not!
It was my Jesus who paid the bail.
Used his own blood, to remove us from hell.
To know my model citizen!
Who could it be?

My God sent down His only son, down here to die for me.
How do we repay that?
In this sin filled world. I only want to speak this truth
To these young boys and girls!
With even knowledge for my elders, I'm beyond my time.
Jesus was persecuted, though he was only living right.
I'm spreading the good news,
Renewed by this faith.
By my God will only continue to shine bright.
Even from this dark place

What If 5-22-11

What if my Jesus was already here?
Waiting for the correct time to start the show
Not Mary nor his closest disciples could see,
So how is it that we would know!
Just here taking a final tally
A recording of all of our actions.
Looking for the church without blemish
Before declaring the final rapture!

What is it that he would say to you?
If he was disguised as a bumb out on the street?
If She was here with me in prison,
Who could say that they even took the time out to visit?
Or even said a simple hello to me.
Sent words of encouragement, or commensary for me to eat?
If my Jesus was lying on the street
Could you honestly say you looked to lend a helping hand?
What if He was in a daycare? Joyously with the kids making friends.
If He was a student in the Detroit public school system
That just got closed down.
A Flint day care, with a sign that reads,
"Do not drink the water." problems underground.
What would She report to the Father
About how we are down here living right now!
Maybe He's that janitor! Working in Grady J. Porter.
Would He be able to say that our Judges and lawyers are working
From truly perfect order!
Possibly He's that father,
Just laid off from his 9-5.
With no way to feed his family, when the corporate executives
Pockets continue to rise.

Could She be that veteran with one leg and one eye?
Who gave her all to serve her country,
Only to be paid back, by being tossed to the side.
If He came back lowly , who is it that would not see?
Only when She started to perform miracles
Then would you decide to believe?
What if my Jesus were here?
Posing as you or me?
What is the report that He would give back?
After the angels finished singing
My God told us before He left:
To love your neighbor as you love me
And above all else, to give all honor to the King.

Whispering In God's Ear 05-27-11

Catch me down on my luck,
Wondering who it is that I can call.
Just needing a little help;
A small lift off.
When my strength just isn't enough,
Who is it that can support me?
My mother? My father?
Friends or family!
If I could dial just one phone number,
Then who's number would it be?
Be it help with a couple of dollars,
Or just an ear that will listen to me.
As I vent out my frustrations
Who will truly listen without judging the inner me?
Never too busy,
Or criticizing of the inward thoughts of me.
What will you do that's inspirational!
Who will dare to listen to my soul,
Relaxing into the depths, that none others will dare to go?
Whether we sit here face to face,
Or if I'm crying into the phone.
Who cares to enter?
Daring to know the length of my mind when it's all alone.
No matter how long it takes,
Willing to give me the precious resource of their time.
Who is it that I can trust?
Allowing them to probe the deep recesses of my grind
Those items that to the surface can break,
And those that I still try to keep froze.

If I would confide in any person
Then who would it be?
One who will take the time out to listen,
And show that they truly love me.
I think someone is already listening.
Deep into the soul of me. Never judgmental,
Content with just allowing me to be me.
From a whisper to a scream
What is it that will make you hear?
I think I feel better,
Thank you for lending me your ears.

This Aint Cool 05-21-2011

So many of yall see this as funny.
Like prison is the cool place to be.
This is no rite of passage!
There are much better places you could be:
Lost in my Fathers house,
Never trying to leave.
Somewhere on a college school yard
Chasing a university degree.
You're wasting a life, long before
It ever got the chance to be.
Technically, I am no better!
Just take a look at me
In the exact same place, as I tell you not to be.
At the humble age of 30,
I know we must make the best of this thing.
Out of here we must remain.
This concentration camp aint no game;
Not a fair field of play!
This is regicide of the new age;
America is blatantly killing us away.
Everybody won't rap,
And we all can't be hoop stars.
Take this time and figure it out
What is your talent?
Gift given from God?
Whatever you did that got you here,
As you see it aint of God.
How many times are you willing to
Come back for drugs and guns!
You see that this aint working!

Don't wait too long,
Or you'll be 60 something years old
Still looking for that same ole song.
When your life is half gone,
And your stuck wondering what to do.
Ask me for advice,
And I will tell you the harsh truth.
Only because I care.
I've done time away, and you
Really do not want to go there!
This shit aint cool.
Is all I can tell ya.
I pray that You'll listen,
Is all I can tell ya.

Can't Knock The Hustle

My Lord sent me much inspiration for the church.
But the Romans went and threw it all away!
Expecting for me to get mad, or for my faith to break.
I just count it all joy, because these words all
Come from the Lord.
Can't remember what the tablet's read from yesterday,
But today, will My Lord not send me some more?
Persistance is the only way.
These evil spirits will not win.
Now I ship these poetics on the underground railroad,
And know that His Angels will safely guide them in.
Here's a message in a bottle
Not carried by delivery pigeons,
But on the backs of doves.
No matter how much this evil world attempts to take away,
We must never give up!
Only moving froward, just day by day
Strength to only move forward, All in faith!
To be cunning as the serpent, but knowing that it is
Doves that leads the way!
Wanting this bride to give up,
But, for the groom, we patiently wait!
Knowing that the day when She comes back,
These evil doers will meet their doom!
Can't knock the hustle, no matter what it is
That you try to do.
We will only come back harder!
No way will our faith you consume.
We are the rulers of the world!
satan stand behind me dude.

This faith cannot be broken.
No matter the evil plot's you throw our way.
Will never stop proclaiming the Word,
No matter how much you try to take my voice away.
Screaming His name loud from the rooftop
Of Jackson state penitentiary.
Catch me behind enemy lines, but refusing to back down.
Continuing to exhault the name of my Lord
Even with all of these evil spirits gathered around.
Take away my Lord's word.
I only hope that you read it!
When the time comes that Jesus comes back, you're gonna need it.

-Wrote after the Jackson state pen took a batch of positive
poems---Thank You! for the inspiration.

Through The Fire 05-22-2011

Tempered and tested
Until the Lord says that it is done.
My God is not bounded by my time limits,
Of our time She knows none.
From the beginning He's been plotting this strategy.
Ever since satans first drawback.
For all we know, their beef may even be from way before that.
Like Job,
She allows satan to bother us and only stand's back.
Stepping in when we're ready to quit, and then He'll ask,
"Do you know the ordinances of the heavens? Can you set their
Dominion over the Earth? look to Pleiades and Orion."
As She points.
"Who created those!"
Our small problems are insignificant,
To the creator of it all.
We have to put selfish gain aside
And just repeat, Through it all....
Yeah, I learned to trust in Jesus.
I learned to give God my all.
Remember that our most pressing times,
Are only for a season, and will pass by as quick as they fall.
God allows us to be tested by fire
Although we may not know the reason why!
Never more than we can handle,
Just keep your eyesight fixed on Jesus in the sky.
"I will never leave you nor forsake you,"
Just look at Hebrews 13:5.
If you need to see it to believe it!
How many can you recall who were tested by fire?
Yet patiently waited for the glory
Just read the end of His story.

My God will add life unto you!
Adding more years onto His glory.
Giving back a hundred times what was lost,
When we only remain faithful to Him.
It's only after we endure the fire,
That Her tender mercies are given.

-Those who bless God in their trials will be blessed by God through their trials.

Part of being authentic is actively living your purpose. Surround yourself with people who encourage you to be who you were meant to be

Mastering Law Of Attraction

To Be Obedient

Heed the voice,
And listen to the call of the Lord
The Holy Spirit lives within us,
We are the kingdom of the Lord
For pain or for pleasure, is it to Her that we will listen?
So many times we don't know why
Directly into resistance, it feels like She's sending us.
Wanting to be comfortable,
But look to My Lord.
Had no will to smile,
Until He got back home to be with God.
Who is it that will be resilient?
Refusing to listen.
It took Jonah a deep storm,
And three days in the belly of a fish for him to listen.
How many of us didn't listen? And watched life go all wrong?
Wanting it to be different,
Feeling that we wrote this same sad song.
Well God is the composer, and Jesus orchestrates.
It is God that is the Potter! We are merely the clay!
Jesus to be the furnace, that solidifies our soul
Takes us from this wicked place,
Allowing that back to God we can go.
How long must it take, before you'll heed the lesson?
At times we find that it's the places that we didn't want to go
That we receive our biggest blessing.
To always think positive, and turn every disavdantage into an
Advantage.
Those who bless God in their trials
Through their trials, will by God, be granted a blessing!
All we must do is endure!

Be willing to go the extra mile.
It is when life becomes the darkest
That we are so close to the light.
For Jesus,
God made the brightest hour of the day void of light.
Once the light returned, The story was all done.
Gone to Her Fathers house,
Preparing the way that you and me have won.

Dancing In The Rain 05-28-2011

Life is full of storms!
Situations where good intents go bad,
And what are we to do? Stand around looking sad?
It takes some lemons to make lemonade!
Dark clouds can block the sun, therefore, making shade.
The reign in the clouds will create rainbows!
volcanic eruptions are needed to create ocean floor.
Every disadvantage can hold an advantage
Only if properly heeded.
Never will we cry and die, just continue with positive proceedings
Be not overcome by evil, but overcome evil with good.
There's always one up.
Just calm your mind to do good.
Discouragement won't be an option, when working by God's Plan.
If the first attempt doesn't go right, then smile
And create a new game plan.
For every attack, what is the counterattack?
The way to give God the glory.
Who could ever sulk,
Knowing that Jesus already accomplished His glory?
Ben Franklin made history!
Simply by standing in the reign.
When thunderstorms come,
No time to frown,
Grab out the umbrella and reign boots,
And go out and dance in the reign with a smile!

This one is for you Ariel Talia Jones my rain dancing buddy!

I love You,

Dad.

Want To Know More 05-28-2011

I sit here with the lights off
As my captor's peer inside.
"What's this light we see?"
They come forth with squinted eyes.
Arms covering the face, almost as if blind.
I only continue to sit here,
Yearning for the soul that rised.
"What's this light we see?"
They begin again.
It is only I
With the great I Am who flows within.
Protected by my holy friend. What do you see?
"What's this light we see."
They just don't understand!
This has nothing to do with electricty,
Or the mind's of men.
"What's this light we see?"
They continue to implore,
And finally I stand up, and move toward the door.
"What's this light we see?" They begin again
Retreating and cowering
Not sure exactly who I Am.
It is only I, and I Am Him.
Because I believe in Him, She does
Even greater works through me.
"What's this light we see?"
And the barred door is no more
What the Father opens,
No man shall close anymore.
They knell in awe, wanting to know more.
I open the book,
And together we begin to explore.

Praise Louder

A wise woman once said,
"Why cheer so loud to a TV that can't even hear you?"
Going rabbid at a sports event, lungs all tired!
From spades games, to chess, to poker we will come to life.
Gossiping to friends, or entertaining a crowd at night.
We will crackle like crazy,
But not praise God aloud!
The one who can hear a whisper
Anytime or anywhere it abounds
All of our praise should go to Her;
Dancing and shouting without a care.
If your inner-most desire depended upon you
Would you stand up and get out of your own way?
Or just stand there looking blue?
Praise God for better days
Praise as if the miracle has already been received;
We just waiting for fruition, but it's already been retrieved.
Speak those things that be not as though they were.
Our thoughts, written and spoken will be.
Will bring our creations to birth
Just you wait and see.
How do we get birth without the labor?
A child that's born premature.
Will have less of a chance of survival
So let's nuture our seeds til' full.
Many great plant's will die, only to be replanted later.
Nuture your creative process
By giving all praise to the creator.

Just Waiting For The Storm To Pass 05-29-2011

I Am the alpha and Omega.
The beginning and the end.
There are many things that must still come to pass.
You only pray that this was the end!
Finding major storms, in places where they weren't before.
You still have time to repent,
Before I open the rest of these doors.
Souls stuck in Hades, just begging for some help.
There's no way for these angels to cross over,
You should have done it before you left.
Why is it that my soldiers don't worry?
Like Jesus they only sleep.
The rest of the congregation continues to pray;
Down on bended knee!
Not for us, but for those stuck outside.
Wanting to only come in, but refusing to swallow their pride.
This world is so full of sin.
Some only think about what they eat
Well I Am the bread of life; Dig in and eat.
What is the atmosphere, when the Father speaks?
Thunder and lightning.
Rumbling in the sky from the east!
The world concerns with computers,
And wanting to know will the banks be alright.
This will all be of no use to thee
When the great I Am comes back to claim life.

Do Not Worry About Tomorrow 05-29-2011

"Therefore I say to you, do not worry about your life. What you will eat; Or about the body, what you will put on. Life is more than food, and the body is more than clothing."

Luke 12:22-23

Today is sufficient for it's own worries
Tomorrow aint guaranteed to beat today.
How could I kill myself
Worrying about what might happen in the next few days?
Trying to fix what I did yesterday!
Stress to be our number one killer in America!
Guns and cancer a thing of the past,
It's your own mind that will bury ya!
We've beat so many of his diseases;
That he had to bring a new illusion to pass.
Worried about how long I may live,
Or how long the money I have in the bank will last.
Worried about what to eat,
When the freezer couldn't fit another steak.
Concerned about my car, and I just bought it today.
Worried about what college my daughter will go to,
And she's only two years old.
Anxious about the rent, and how to pay the electricty.
When the fish and bread wasn't enough,
Jesus simply said, "Here, give me those."
Gave thanks for it to his Father
And put the disciples to work.
Handing out the little bits and pieces!
Then collecting all of the leftovers from the earth.
Only live for today! Give Her the little two's and fews.
Watch as he gives thanks to the Father,
And hands a whole multitude back unto you!

Simply look at the birds!
All of the small animals running along the ground.
And no matter the season,
All you will be able to do is smile.
Be thankful for everything!
Don't allow the evil one to decieve you!
It may never look like enough,
But my God will even perform small miracles for you too!
Only live for today! Find any way to smile.
Tomorrow aint guaranteed. My Jesus came down.
Paid us all a visit
What was His report back to the crown!
Are you horting what She gave onto you?
Or smiling, and joyously sending your lil bit back around?

Boycott The Prisons 05-29-2011

I can't even look you up on the stock index!
How to put you out of business?
No more of the bad food,
In-humane treatment, or tortuous living conditions!
From asbestos, mold to mildew, where is the inspector?
Maybe he's not allowed in here;
For her such as blessing!
The sinks don't work, and what's this corrode that grows within?
I'm supposed to drink plenty of water to help my blood pressure
But how do I drink this?
Is this brown stuff rust?
And why so many legs on that dust?
I've never seen nothing like this!
A little paint and some curtains,
And maybe even Martha couldn't fix this dump up.
This abandoned building, doesn't even have heat ducts.
How do inmates make it through the Michigan winters?
With no Michigan energy trucks?
My toilet is holding on to something,
And I'm not quite sure how it knows my name.
How long has it been here is my next question?
Because the sanitizer even runs away.
I know we are all just inmates, criminals. A number!
But I was a human before this.
Boy! You have no rights,
Once you have on this orange and blue jumper.
Well how do I give you back this?
It doesn't even fit me anymore.
Most will never understand! And I'm happy for you.
But for the other half of Michigan's population,
What are we supposed to do?

Well I've been sent on the inside,
And I Am still scared to let my hands touch myself.
When it is that I came in here. I had a clean bill of health.
From mercia to hepititis,
Syphliss to HIV,
How do I know what has been grafted right onto me;
No sterilization of these mats! Just let the filth breed.
My antibacterial soap aint enough for that!
Even clorox has fleed.
How about we trade places? Just for a few hours.
I think part of a judges training,
Should be for them to do some time behind bars.
How many months would the prosecutor recommend?
If they was housed right next to me?
How many special pardons would the govenor give?
If she sat right here next to me!
I know, he's not the criminal!
That all depends on the lenz from which you see.
An A.P.B. to parents, churches,
Skools we cannot count on the government!
We must do what we have to do, to see this cease.
Whatever it is! We must go out and save our kids!
Give them something to do long before they ever reach this!

The Sacrifice 05-29-2021

"Those who are well have no need of a physician, but those who are sick. I have not come to call the righteous, but sinners, to repentance."

Luke 5:31-32

Who else could sit amongst those, cast out by society?
Sinners and tax collectors!
When only the best of life is bottled up inside of me.
Ministering to the murderers and rapist!
Who else is there that can see?
Child molesters and tax evaders!
Now who else would volunteer, but the king!
Drunkend drivers and armed robbers,
We all need to be saved.
God is merciful in forgiving,
Even those our society cast away.
Discarded like garbage! Still useful in the heavenly kingdom.
The high ups in society may look down on em
But what will Jesus go through in order to lift us up with Him?
Just to make certain that one soul get's saved?
No body can claim to be perfect, we all need to be saved.
How far are you willing to go,
To save a soul that may be falling away?
Each day we pass one,
But how many of us will just look in the other way?
Feeling that one is beneath you,
Or that one doesn't deserve to be saved.
My Jesus jumped right in! Never flinched or turned away.
How can I be afraid of my own kind?
When it is His power that lights the way?
The devil loves the fact that I wont lose mine,
In order for yours to save.

He that looses his own life......
We daily bear the cross by faith!!
Going in to take our stuff back, no matter what it may take.
The way I got here is real significant,
But what's more important is how I will come away.
He who believes shall do much greater things than these
Head held high, I walk back into the devils parade.
Believeing that when the time is right
My God will bring me away.
Those who have been given to me! None are gone astray!
The son of perdition, served his purpose,
And now his time is done.
No way will we be afraid! Only believe! Says Mark 36.
This power has been given by God.
Her strength proves perfect when I am weak.
How could He come down to this layer,
When He right now dwells with the king?
How would He wear these shackles, when She was born free?
No one engaged in warfare, entangles himself with
The affairs of me!
If my God told me too!
You'd find me wandering in the wilderness for 40
Days and nights too!
Though I walk through the valley of the shadow of death
I shall fear no evil.
What you see inside of me is my Father's light.
He looked down for one that He knew He could send,
And I stood up. "I AM he."
Put me through training to be here! Knowing that I had to come.
Saving these souls is more important than my paycheck,
I Am my Fathers son.
Don't feel sorry for me! Just know that I must go.
Continue to hope and pray for me,
Until the day my God opens the door.

She Who Overcomes 05-30-2011

"And he who overcomes, and keeps my works until the end, to him
I will give power over the nations."
Revelation 2:26

Hold fast to your faith,
And steadfastly mount up on wings like eagles.
It's not by me or you,
But by patience that we will receive this.
Can you see yourself dressed in all white,
Name jotted in the book of life?
Free from the hour of trial.
Heading toward eternal life!
She who drinks from this well, will never go thirsty again.
To be a pillar in His Temple;
Never to leave from this kingdom again.
By my Jesus! Refined by the fire.
Chastened, in order to enter through that door,
To sit at the left or the right of Him;
Who will first drink from the cup that He has poured?
And then just like Jesus, She'll lift me up!
Don't worry about the trials!
Have joy in tribulations! Never giving up.
My Jesus already overcame.
No matter the dark hour that we may be facing.
Count it all joy!!
Reverened Howell I can still see your smiling face,
Still studying your spin move,
Landing in the same space.
It's not even first sunday yet, and with the hidden manna we ate.
Knowing I'm not even worthy,
Such the sinner I am in this consecrated space.
Can you imagine sitting in the sunset,
Eating from the tree of life?

In paradise with the king! My God promises eternal life.
And His word never lies,
Just continuing to be patient.
Relieving the mind of all doubt..
All according to His orchestrating,
Is the only way that we will make it!
Do not fear any of those things which you are about to suffer!
I am the root and the offspring of David,
The bright and morning star.

"But you are those who have continued with me in my trials and I bestow upon you a kingdom, just as my Father bestowed one upon me."

Luke 22:28-29

Come and See 05-30-2011

"And Nathaniel said to him, "Can anything good come out of
Nazareth?" Phillip said to him, "Come and See.""

From high crime and incarceration rates,
Skyrocketing homelessness and foreclosure rates.
No casinos this way, and GM had to close up it's doors.
Drug dealers and prostitutes walking up and down Kalamazoo!
No peace on Dr. Martin Luther King Jr. Blvd.
The government steady cutting back on needs for the schools.
Stealing the teachers pensions, and firing the fire department And
Police too!
What's the relation to Gotham city?
And we don't have nearly as many people as you.
Government bonuses! When the people down here starving!
Where's our dark night?
We need a batman to get to the heart of this:
Drugs always in demand; Military guns in the hands of our kids.
"Can anything good come out of Nazareth?"
Come and See.
Babies even out here starvin; Left at the hospital for adoption.
Another Brenda just cut an umbilical cord;
Another baby found thrown in the garbage.
"Can anything good come out of Nazareth?"
Come and see.
Another Brother just got murdered in cold blood,
Right there on the street.
Churches closing, homeless shelters folding
Mothers with kids living in houses with no heat!
"Can anything good come out of Nazareth?"
Come and See.

Bankruptcy and short sales,
The banks dont even want these properties no more.
No college funding, but let the prisons
Fill up their doors.
With social security as the next to go,
"Can anything good come out of Nazareth?"
I just need to know. Point me in the right direction,
Which way next is the best way I should go?
"Can anything good come out of Nazareth?"
Come and See.

If they not giving you energy putting a battery in your back let
them go! Friends/family/relationship or business! No fear

Meek Mill

To Just Hear You 05-30-2011

I can hear these voices in my head,
Not exactly sure whose they may be.
One telling me something, while another disagrees with He.
Which one is the truth? Who is leading me wrong and who Right?
Then along comes a third, possibly my own insight.
Just weighing out the options,
Until I hear my family and friends.
Which voice am I to live by?
Then the first two start back up,
And it all starts all over again.
A battle within this soul. To which I AM a total stranger
Still thinking which way should we go?
To put an end to this anger;
Sanity? In the midst of such danger!
Which one do we listen to?
They all make valid points.
Then I remember the saying,
From an old native man:
"There's a war going on inside of you,
between two opposing sides;
The one that you feed will live,
The one that you starve will die."

Allow Me To Speak To Your People 05-31-2011

"And suddenly a voice came from heaven, saying, "This is my
Beloved Son, in whom I am well pleased." Matt 3:17

Thank you Lord for allotting me this gift;
Allowing me to speak to your people!
Using your word to provide this lift.
Just a little inspiration, to those that may need it.
Hanging on to your truth!
No matter how many may not receive this.
Proclaiming of Jesus' Resurrection,
Only you can bring back the dead from the dirt.
You are our resurrection!
Giving us a second chance here on earth.
Jesus began his ministry, around the age of 30,
Will you be using me to proclaim your ministry?
After all that's happened in my story,
Believing I was the reason for the good of it all.
You let me fall flat on my face, then pruned me.
Now I know that all of this glory be to God!
You are my reason for believing,
Even when I don't have a dollar in my pocket.
You are the reason to keep achieving!
Even while paying the consequences for my falling.
How do we never get discouraged,
Even when the world gives us plenty of reasons to?
Just keep your head held high!
Mind stayed on Jesus Christ the whole way through.

"Do not be afraid, but speak, and do not be silent; For I Am with
you, and no one will attack you to hurt you; For I have many people
in this city."

ACTS 18:10

Ye Are gods 05-30-2011

"If they do not know, nor do they understand; They walk
about in darkness; All the foundations of the earth are unstable."
Psalm 82:5

This is not an attempt to take any power from the King,
Or to step on my Jesus's feet!
Psalm 82:6 spells it out with a lowercase G.
Are we pitiful, or are we powerful?
Of the word we must understand.
If She is the whole beach, then you are a grain of sand.
Simply a pool from an ocean,
You have the same contents as She.
Yes you can cast out demons,
But only according to your level of belief.
If you hold your thoughts to Godly standard,
Then your physical must live up to the same.
Yes we are all sinners, but thank Jesus
That we can be born again.
He who provides us with this power,
Does declare all of the glory.
There is nothing man can do without He;
Just another whithered branch,
Headed into a scorching.
Let the flames come onto us!
He will blow them away.
Already proving we won't be charred by the fire
When He leads our way.
To know of your current value,
And then to exceede the expectations.
When the mind is stayed on Jesus,
It's not as difficult as we may sometimes believe it is to make it.
Yeah, I had to get refined!
But look at me now.

Like a diamond in the rough, you are gold;
Personally polished by the Crown!
Until the refiner can see His reflection,
She will keep you in the heat;
At extreme and unbearable temperatures!
No matter how long it may take to melt thee.
See Her with tongs in hand, welding mask on face!
Only She knows how high your temperature needs to go,
The exact amount of temperature!
That perfect amount of pressure that the process will take.
Don't be ashamed of what it took,
Or of what you had to go through to take your seat!
My past is not what my future holds
Thank you Stevie Wonder for what you allowed me to see.
Ye are gods!
No matter what this world may say.
Put your power to use
And put satan in his place.

"Is it not written in your law, I said you are gods."
John 10:35

Do What You Are Told 05-31-2011

"Cast the net on the right side of the boat, and you will find some."
John 21:6

How many times have you cast all night?
Not catching one fish.
Exhausted and tired by daylight,
Just wanting to call it quits.
Have you ever been told to travel somewhere?
That you really did not want to go?
Begrudingly you depart, looking for the reasons to say no.
What if you were told to lead a people?
None of which wanted to listen to you:
Consistently yelling into a microphone,
While they only complain about food.
When have you ever been told to give something away?
That you held dear to heart
Will you willingly pass it on?
Or find a viable substitute with which to depart?
Where would you put your faith?
If you couldn't see what you were told to believe?
Making our own graven images, out of tangible things.
Who is it that you will listen to?
If I told you to do something in which you didn't know how?
Why would you keep the faith
Even through all of the laughter, mockery and trials?
In this world, so many walk by sight,
Rather than leaping out on faith!
Thank you God! That we are not of this crooked place!
Just aliens and foreigners,
Like E.T. waiting to go home.
Living lowly here, anticipating going back to my heavenly Throne.

Only here to save others! Show them the Godly way.
Overcoming our circumstances; Jesus already overcame.
What just seems to be too dificult?
Being whispered by that voice deep within your soul?
Jump out of the plane without a parachute!
And on His wings,
Like an eagle you will soar.

I'll Never Be A Prisoner 06-01-2011

Don't call me an inmate!
I am surely a hostage.
Held here against my will.
You be America, And I will be an American Indian.
What kind of consecration camp is this?
New age slavery!
And this here is one big boat.
Sell me to the highest bidder, "Look this one's big and strong."
Not about Re-entrance into society,
But how much the federal government
Is willing to pay for us;
I see children in here 16 years old!
Who will never again see the light of day with us.
What kind of world are we living in?
No, car jacking aint pretty,
But what are you doing to save me?
Cutting schools, and reducing teacher pay!
Close down the Boys and girls clubs
For the sake of coroprate pay.
Where are all of my role models?
Any hero to come and save the day.
These are America's seeds!
Instead of helping them we claim to be afraid.
My Grandmother would have taken her belt off,
But you're right, this is a whole new day.
Child protective services, to even locking me away.
Then when my teen drops out of school,
Or becomes a threat to society
All of the burdon is thrown right back upon me.
Right upon my head, all the weight will lay.
You need to take responsibility!

For this monster you've created.
I know you don't feel bad; This world has gone to satan.
And you are all his kids! Romans times 10!
All about financial gain.
This world is in some real deep shit.
Look to me as a new age Jesus,
Just trying to help you change your ways.
Slaughter me if you want to.
Watch what my Father does to this space.
I Am only a prisoner of Jesus Christ! How about you?
If She called for the heavens to part right now,
Then where would you be?
What you do unto one of these, you also do onto me.
Sit up on that bench, all high and mighty
When it's time for us all to answer,
Then it is that we'll see,
Never to be a prisoner.
Simply a soldier for G-O-D.

Bring It To The Alter 06-01-2011

"Fools and blind! For which is greater, the gold or the temple that
sanctifies the gold."
Matthew 23:17

Misery and heartache, anger and despair.
Hair loss, and kidney problems
High blood pressure! Don't go there.
Diabeties to thyroid problems,
Miracles happen everyday.
Bitterness and disappointment will not just fade away.
Bring it to the alter!
Not once but everyday.
Bring it to the alter!
Until you can finally say that it's gone away.
New jobs and inheritance
Domestic issues to pass away.
Getting up from your sick bed
When the Doctors claimed you would pass away.
No more cancer or frustration!
Yes there is a cure for herpes.
When all else said it to be impossible,
How many would not give up on faith and belief?
When this life just aint fair,
But we deal with it anyway.
Placing all faith in She; Who is now gone away,
But promised to come back at a later date.
Bring it to the alter!
And I bet She'll meet you there.
Bring it to the alter
She's probably already there.

How many of God's soldiers were thrown into imprisonment?
For whatever the reason:
Well, Joseph was falsely acused of rape;
Sampson was enemy of the philistines;
Jehoiachin and Zedekiah were held political captives;
Jeremiah was kept away from his people;
John the Baptist spoke out against Herod,
Marrying his brothers wife;
Peter belonged to the church;
Paul and Silas were thrown in,
For preaching the Gospel of Christ;
Paul was preaching to God's people!!
Can you see Daniel locked away in that den of lions?
Scared or confident? Held against his will.
How could I ever feel bad,
Being in the company of such great men.
They all never gave up faith in the Lord,
So found good favor from Him.
No matter how long they were put in
It only strengthened the bond with God day by day.
Can you imagine being thrown into a miry pit?
And patiently waiting on the hand of the Lord to make a way?
My A-Team did many years in prison
Yet only served every day.
Through it all just continued to remain faithful
Hearing God right on through the release date.

Please Don't Let me Die 06-01-2011

Locked away in this cage, for none else to see!
After being gone for so long,
How will my people remember me?
As a fighter? As a soldier? As a son of the Lord?
As a sinner? As a thief? Need I say more.
Who will keep me alive, although I'm dead to the world?
Send a picture to my daughter,
Child support to my girls!
What will be my legacy?
Will the internet capture my glory?
Another great has fallen;
Smile and say cheese.
Goodness covered up by madness,
Critics find joy in the folly.
Pointing fingers and clowning, "I'm glad he's gone away."
Maybe he'll stay in the valley
To never again see the rise of a new day!
Avoid the humiliation and heartache.
Never rise again. I can hear the melody singing:
Is this the end?
No more of me!
"And he was such a good kid." What a tragedy;
Slum body posture and headshakes after this.
Hero's get remembered, but legends never die.
I'm fallen to the son of perdition.
See these tears in my eyes!
Kneeling to the cross like Sampson,
Just give me one more try.
To bring vengence unto thine enemies
Yes! I'm only a man!
Wanting to be immortal.
Your word says to live forever, I can?

How long will be eternity?
When is it too late,
To catch that train ride into heaven?
To sleep an eternal sleep
And rise no more.
I see Gabriel coming down to get me.
Just not yet prepared,
To walk through that opened door.
Don't let me die here.
Away from the ones that I love
Just keep the light shining,
Flames from the heavenly won above.

My Heart Sings Unto the Lord   06-02-2011

"Sing to the Lord, for He has triumphed gloriously! The horse and it's rider He has thrown into the sea. The Lord is my strength and song, and He has become my salvation."

Exodus 15: 1-2

How would I not make a joyful noise?
Knowing that it is Her goodness that redeemed me.
Sing out the honor of Her name;
Make Her praise glorious. Saints sing!
You may ask what we sing about:
I will sing of mercy and justice;
To you, O Lord I will sing praises.
Make a joyful shout to the Lord all you lands!
Serve the Lord with gladness;
Come before His presence with singing.
For those who carried us away captive, asked of us a song,
And those who plundered us requested mirth,
saying, "Sing us one of those songs of Zion!"
How shall we sing the Lord's song in a foreign land?
If I forget you, O Jerusalem, let my right hand forget its skill!
Behold, my servants shall sing for joy of heart,
But you shall cry for sorrow of heart, and wail for grief of spirit.
I will pray with the spirit,
And I will also pray with the understanding.
I will sing with the spirit,
And I will also sing with the understanding.
I will declare your name to my brethren;
In the midst of the assembly I will sing praise to you.
Is anyone among you suffering? Let him pray.
Is anyone cheerful? Let him sing psalms.
The singers went before,
The players on instruments followed after;
Among them were the maidens playing timbrels

Bless God in the congregations,
The Lord from the fountain of Israel.
There is little benjamin, their leader;
I acquired male and female singers,
The delights of the sons of men.
And musical instruments of all kinds.
Then our mouth was filled with laughter,
And our toungue with singing.
Then they said among the nations,
The Lord has done great things for them.
The flowers appear on the earth; The time of singing has come,
And the voice of the turtledove is heard on our land.
The whole earth is at rest and quiet;
They break forth into singing.
It shall blossom abundantly and rejoice,
Even with joy and singing
The glory of Lebanon shall be given to it,
The excellence of Carmel and Sharon
And the ransomed of the Lord shall return,
And come to Zion with singing,
With everlasting joy in their heads.
They shall obtain joy and gladness,
And sorrow and sighing shall flee away.
For the fruit of the spirit is in all goodness,
Righteousness, and truth.
Speaking to one another in Psalms and Hymns
And spiritual songs,
Singing and making melody in your heart to the Lord,
Giving thanks always for all things to God the Father
In the name of our Lord Jesus Christ.

Disclaimer: Only .05% of these lines are my own. The other 95% are from the book of my Lord! Masked together into a poetic masterpiece which only He could create meaning! Dare to find them in the good book, or will you simply believe me?

Why'd You Take me Away 06-03-2011

Excuse me Mr. Canady:
If I could oblidge a moment of your time.
Just want to talk to you about my sentencing.
You gave your opinion and now here is mine:
I know you're out to form your reputation,
Of making criminals pay!
I know my crime was strong, way unlike my way.
There's others, on paper, who deserve more,
But you so decided to max out on me!
Repeat offenders, and pedifiles on teether!
Yet you incarcerate me for more:
Back in school, and starting a business!
What's the true meaning of corrections?
I live with regret each and every day
Wondering what happens if the right house was hit that day?
I made a decision well beyond my morals,
And that is truly not what I Am about.
A lapse of judgement, A brain fart!
Guess you're giving me some time to think it out.
I'll make the best of this living,
Because God lives strong in me.
How many can still do the right thing;
For me, right by Cogswell St.
To help or to hinder? What were you out to do may 11 2009!
Got the feeling to please the world,
In hopes that they will reelect you when it's time.
But I'll take this time, because it fits the crime,
Although this wasn't the agreement.
Like Joseph, I've been sold into bondage,
But my God will use this for His advantage.
To sit on that bench, and claim to be afraid of me!
Proves you don't know me as you should.

But I pray that when the day comes, and it's hell to pay
My Father will have mercy and forgive as He should.
My enemies shall be my footstool
Those who've held captive shall be the captives.
I'll hold no bitterness, or hold no grudge
God knows the heart of me so my mind is at peace.
He's told me take up my bed and walk
Yet sin no more,
Or your punishment will be times ten!!
To Cogswell St! My heart goes out to you everyday
I pray that you forgive
By the strength of the Lord we will trip this negative
And create a positive for the young boys and girls from it.

Be your own biggest fan, your own biggest believer, and put it on your back and carry that weight.

Nipsey Hustle

For Keeping Me Inspired 06-03-2011

When it looked like all the chips had fallen down;
All hope was lost.
Some of you still believed; The select few.
Cheering me on through life, screaming,
"You can make it out."
Punch drunk and knees shaking,
looking heavily sedated.
Not knowing which way to go.
Feeling that there was no way left to shake it.
Hoping that this life would go right;
Rather face death.
Health is what I hoped would never come back to me.
Listening to naysayers telling me to plead insanity
As my best bet.
Take out a law suit, on the Indiana State Police?
They thought this life was gone: Didn't know the true me.
Born to be a winner!
Even after falling flat on my face.
No foul up is too big, for my God's saving grace.
Thanks to all of those who told me, this wasn't the end.
Only to hold my head up high!
To dare to get in the ring again.
Well this time I found a new trainer
My Gus is my Lord. Spent overtime in my Father's house,
Just re-reading the word.
My God is the master healer, to those that repent.
Bow down to the cross, and confess your sin.
She wiped my tears away, only saying pick up my bed;
Your sins have been forgiven, just don't do this again.
Now I spend my time away; Repayment to the world.
I Am not from here!
Even in here you'll find my Lord.

Re-attaching my soul
Engrafting my life to He.
Said everything we do shall prosper.
Thank you to all that believe!
To the rest why bother?
Even your hate inspires me.
Using this all for fuel,
And inspiration to achieve.

The day is new
Still the laborers are few
These children won't listen
What are we supposed to do?

To see the truth
We look for you!
Noticing the goodness
That comes with you.

To speak the truth
We search for you,
Reading through chapters
Again and again.

What will I see new?
That will rekindle
Your fire from within?
Bringing the newness in, fresh and new

The passing of everyday
Is but a new learning stage.
Allowing me to see
What your people need to hear.

What else to do?
But spend my time with you
Coming to your mount again and again
Just looking to find some truth.

In the world of sin
How do we consecrate?
To be released
From the filth of sin?

Absolve me once,
Clean me twice,
How many times must you clean me
Before I am dead to this sin filled life?

We need fresh word today
So what am I to do?
I speak one to one with Jesus
He's my best friend through and through!

Not where I Am going
Nor where I have been,
But for the present
To only rely on the Him.

To keep the mind focused,
Only on the cross.
Jesus paid the price
Thus my soul has been bought.

Of all the lives He bought.
Will you take the credit?
Or flee another day?
Continuing to give the credit unto satan.

We know who wins, to hell I've been
And smacked satan right in the face.
God is all! His love stands tall,
Hurry up and claim it before its too late all.

To Make a Living From Prison   06-03-2011

How many can say they got their start in life?
While sentenced to time behind bars?
50 percent tithes to the church,
And an organization in the name of those I've scared.
Yet and still, we live like movie stars.
Donate to the homeless, feed and shelter the war vets.
Delighted to pick up the tab
To which America will never admit.
Thank you God for this talent,
And even more for the people who will read it.
We simply kindling a flame to burn worldwide
In order to give back to those that need it.
Bonuses for my teachers, and supplies for the kids.
This work is not done for me,
But to glorify the name of Jesus,
And live in the light that She gives.
We publish and sell so much positive work
That now even Oprah wants to say Hi.
Couldn't counsel when I needed it,
Now my God provides.
Every disadvantage holds an advantage!
All negatives a positive.
Even from what seems to be a dead end
God will prove a way out of the debacle.
When we just keep believing.
Knowing that we can fly
Don't be afraid to mount your dreams!
No matter how hopeless it may seem,
Nor the obstacles that try to block out the light.
Good things will come, to those who believe.

We just have to train the brain to think positive,
Sit me away for up to five years,
My Lord provides this pay,
And compounded is to be the intrest on it.
Exponential to be the growth that will come from this
Simply to be given away.
It's all for the Lords benefit
That for tomorrow,
I'm earning my living today.

Concentration Camp 06-03-2011

Find us locked in this new age slave ship;
Like chattle we locked down.
The federal government has paid for this property;
Cleaning and fattening us up
Before we're shipped all around.
No longer free, but branded by a six digit number;
satan makes blatant what's his.
You must kill me! Won't iron that onto my skin!
I'm waiting for my Lord to come down to get me.
He marks on the forehead and dresses his children in all white.
You can keep these county blues,
Far from confused,
I know all of my spiritual rights.
You can't steal Its joy; You can take these toys
The kingdom She provides is within:
The screaming and hollering;
Laughter of people.
Like hearing souls in hades screaming trynna get out of this.
They flock like roaches, just keep em flowing
And we'll kill the moral, and spiritual beliefs.
Genocide. No time for races,
Lets just exterminate everything that breathes.
Just pull the plug, show them no love,
Treat them lower than human beings.
They like that and it only ensures that
They'll be right back.

Something Just Happened in Heaven 06-03-2011

Thank you Lord for this feeling,
Although physically I don't know exactly what it is.
My soul keeps screaming out,
Yelling thank you Lord, for whatever it is that you just did.
The windows of heaven have opened!
Upon my head I can feel the blessings you give.
Thank you Lord for allowing these tender mercies
And allowing this time to pass by in but a blip.
Wanting to enjoy the precious seconds,
Yet wanting to be back at home with my girls.
My heart knows that there's a plan you see
That my human mind could never unfurl.
I just place all faith in you,
And thank you for allowing me to carry out your deed.
Just to be a part of this;
Somthing so much bigger than me.
Happy to be your servant;
More than enough for me.
In this warfare, I am just a pawn
Happy to follow your lead.
Proud to be your soldier, an army of won.
The benefits here are much greater
And I know you will never leave me un-done;
Something happened in heaven today, and physically I can't see
Whatever it is I thank you
Because it lit the soul of me!!
Whomever it was for! Doesn't even have to be me
Just glad to hear the angels singing.
Stomping on demons in victory.

"Then Moses answered and said, " But suppose they will not believe me or listen to my voice; suppose they say, 'The lord appeared to you.'"

Exodus 4:1

How far will a messenger of God have to go?
Before the people hear the word as the truth?
A rod turned into a serpent?
Water to become blood, what will make them listen to you?
Maybe if the hand, before the face, turned white as snow.
God I can't do this!
And who would listen while I Am in this place?
Your servant has fallen;
Slipped right out of the race.
Then the Lord proceeded,
"Who has made the ear to hear or the eyes to read?
The mouth to speak? Was not that me?
Now therefore, write, And I will be with your hand
And teach your heart what you shall say."

So the anger of the Lord was kindled:
"Is not Pastor Cotton your leader? I know that She leads well, and look, She is also coming out to meet you. When She sees you, she will be glad in Her heart. Now you shall minister unto him and put the word in his heart. And I will be with
Your heart and with his heart, and I will teach you what you shall Write.
So She shall be your teacher of the word. And he himself shall be as a pupil to you, and you shall speak to him from God.
And you shall take this pen and paper in your hand with which you shall do the signs."

With that I took up this pen.
Blazing through pads of paper.
"Do you know where many wrote their portion of the Bible?
I could hear Her voice taylor?"
With unfailing consistency I pray as I write,
"Please Lord, my God, Just let this come out right."
With He sending me titles any time of day or night.
Even at 3 or 4 in the morning,
He'd summon for my soul to rise.
"What do you want me to say?"
Wiping the crud from my eyes.
Knowing that this is the Holy Spirit,
I'm too tired for it to be me.
With the lights off, I scribble on paper
Untill the voice will instruct:
"Pray. And now I lay me back down to sleep."
Never too much! For this meaning I've been called.
From that day forward, I've given this right hand to God.

Here's to another day on the wakeup list!
For at least one more chance for
The breath of life you give.
Up in the morning, before the dew is gone
And with the birds, my heart begins to sing songs.
Calling on the glorious light to awaken this new thing
True believers know the Son never goes down;
It's still shining just on another scene.
Good morning God, Thank you for kissing my face.
Blowing on my skin, making my soul smile
Taking all of the darkness right up and out of this place.

Coming Back to My Father's House 06-03-2011

"If God will be with me and keep me in this way that I Am going, and give me bread to eat and clothing to put on, so that I come back to my Father's house in peace, then the Lord shall be my God."

Genesis 28: 20-21

When I last left my Fathers house,
My countenance said I may be gone long.
One last kneel at the cross, a final bow to the alter!
Mental pictures of the pulpit, A last smell of these seats.
Taking inventory of the growth to be made, and enjoying the
Beauty that I currently see.
Heart felt hugs and I love yous to my brothers and sisters;
Just wanting to break down and cry.
Tell my soulmate how much I will miss her
Not wanting the people to freak out; To keep my cool, I try.
Lingering in the pastor's office, for one last time!
Looking around the pastor's office
For things I don't even expect to find.
Looking for the proof of faith that we could not find.
The long walk down the separating line.
Through the first set of double doors,
Standing in the entrance way not wanting to step foot
Through the next set of double doors.
This here has come to be my sanctuary. My safe place!
Make the law come and get me!
Drag me outside, tear me from my Father's space,
If you want to take me on a ride upstate.
Stepping out of the exit doors and standing outside
I admire the character of this building;
Love the birds nests in the cross.
Out to the parking lot, me and my soulmate walk.
She urges me along, with love and faith in her eyes.

Feeling my inward difficulties, only wanting me to smile.
We walk over the uneven pavement, hand in hand.
So much I want to say to her,
But I dont want to come off like an unbelieving man.
Like Jesus I must be a sacrifice, and go my Fathers way.
Our circumstances are different.
Different prices we must pay.
He to save the world,
And me, simply to build the peoples faith.
For my sins have already been forgiven,
But two years later,
And now to society I must pay.
I'll take this prison sentence, In the name of the Lord.
You can never take what He put into my heart
No matter how high or low you decide to go!
Tell my Fearless Faith family that I'll be coming home one day.
For now!
I must go away, but I'll be coming home one day

"How lovely is your tabernacle, O Lord of hosts! My soul longs, yes
even faints for the courts of the Lord; My heart and my flesh cry
out for the living God."

Psalm 84:1-2

The Hope is This..... 06-03-2011

"For he who lacks these things is shortsighted, Even to blindness, and has forgotten that he was cleansed from his old sins."

2 Peter 1:9

.....Justice will prevail over injustices
....Where sin abounded mercy abounded much more.
...Disapointment, heartache, anger and maliciousness
Will give way to forgiveness and thanks forevermore!
...He will avenge us our enemies!
That He can hear me when I pray.
His grace is sufficient, just enough for today.
...Our sins are really forgiven,
When we bring them all to Him
And that His angels will light the way.
To overcome evil with the light of Him.
God knows exactly where to find us.
....That His word is good and will do as it should.
Releasing us from strongholds that bind us,
...Jesus is not a myth, but by the Father he rules.
As the shepard, sent here to guide us out,
Show us the correct way, guide us back to light.
...When things don't go our way,
And bad just seems to override the right
It is the Holy Spirit that still guides us.
When we break a covenant with His faith.
There's a way for Him to mend us back
Into the vine of life with His way.
This blazing inferno I Am in,
You've no fear to come in
No matter how hot the heat that blinds us.
Jesus died for our sin
Now we're given a second attempt.
God is truly in His temple

With the earth as his footstool
And his mind stayed on lowly us.
We are only sinners, worms, maggots, and airbenders
The hope is that
She is truly willing to save us.

"But beloved, do not forget this one thing, that with the Lord one day is as a thousand years, and a thousand years as one day. The Lord is not slack concerning Her promise, as some count slackness, but is longsuffering toward us, not willing that any should perish but that all should come to repentance."

2 Peter 3:8-9

Every morning is a fresh beginning everyday is the world made
new today is a new day

I love when they think you are nobody and you turn out to be
the GOAT

EMINEM

9:00 A.M. Callout 06-04-2011

Saturday morning is my favorite day!
Meditating in the tabernacle of my Lord.
Moses told Joshua: "Go out to the Amaleks and make war"!
The whole time he had to hold his arms up;
Rod held high in the sky.
If he got tired and dropped them,
Then his Israelites would die.
Now how long do you think it takes,
For two sides to finish a battle?
I've tried it for 9:00 A.M. call out
And that prayer warrior only lasts for an hour.
Hold your hands high to the sky
The next time your on call out in Fearless Faith.
Envision our members casting out demons
And willing strongholds out of the way.
When I finished,
All I could do was smile.
Listening to the birds go crazy!
When a second before, all was quiet!
We still declaring war, but I aint Moses.
Get in on the 9:00 A.M. callout
Only the few are chosen!
Some will heed the call,
Others will run away.
We front line soldiers!
Like marines trained to clear the way.
Thank God for deacons like the Trippletts
To show us how this is done.
The few and the proud!
We are an army of won.
Behind General Cotton!
We carefully pressing on

Looking on to greatness, with each day of the rising sun.
By training and by fortitude
We get the job done.
Always ready to battle,
Whatever the forces that may come!
For this battle with Jesus,
Are you prepared to lose your life?
Because there is no turning back from this
Once we're charging into this fight.
Be prepared for this warfare!
On call at all times
Even if you don't make it to my Fathers house
Never be late for Saturday morning at 9.

Joy Thiefs 06-04-2011

Close the windows!
Slam the doors!
You the ones miserable.
I'm only here for 30 days,
But you stuck here doing more time than I will in this.
Turn on the air conditioner,
Scream and yell obscene names!
Dont be mad at me,
Because your boss is stripping your retirement away.
My future is secure! Funds stocked by the Lord
The earthly rich man in Hades;
Only pleaded for Lazarus to dip his finger in the water
And cool his sores.
This is the entrance to hell
And you dare to guard its gates?
Doing the devils work, all in the name of pay.
Pop the basketballs, and take away the weights!
This work from my Lord you can never take away.
No need for Tv's and radios
I got studying to do;
Pastor when I grow up, I want to be just like you!
The brain full of addresses,
And ready to proceede with its applications.
In all of your reading,
Remember to get some understanding.
What God gives to us,
The world can't take it away.
Even for those who hold me captive,
I will constantly pray and wish good their way.
You could have no power at all against me
Unless it had been given you from above.

It's hard to love our enemy,
But much easier to love those that we love.
Weaping may endure for a night,
But joy comes in the mourning.
Take whatever it is that you feel like taking from me,
Just know my Lord is coming.
No matter how much you go home and drink,
You cant' drink the rapture away.
Smoke all the coke and cigarettes you want,
But you can still only come to heaven through this way,
Or bye your foolish pride will Peter turn you away?
We refuse to know Jesus,
Playing mind games and pretending to not need the faith;
I see the fear in your face.
Gun range steady popping off shots across the street,
But those in here are not afraid to die.
Your mental scare tactics are all worthless;
Why are you so afraid of me?
No way possible for you to take my joy away,
But willingly,
I'll share with you this joy
God put down deep inside of me.

Against All the Forces of evil 06-04-2011

"We are hard pressed on everyside. Yet not crushed: We are perplexed, but not in despair; Persecuted, but not forsaken; Struck down, but not destroyed."

2 Corinthians 4:8

Centering my gravity, feet anchored into the ground.
evil is forming a mighty attack. I can feel it all around.
Knowing God's forces are stronger; I only embrace,
And prepare for impact;
The Word being the reason for this faith.
The collision is upon us, yet we refuse to stand back.
We push forward with the Angels;
Fighting along side mere men.
From the beginning the worlds have been merging
Now we know that this is close to the end.
Through sweat, tears, and blood we keep fighting till the end.
Pushing the forces away,
Knowing we are the front lines in this.
If we lose these gaps, all others will be forced to pay.
This is a mighty battle! We press deeper into the faith.
Pressing forward inch by inch,
Patiently waiting for the correct time to overtake.
satans power must weaken.
Then in God's name again we will push through.
Envision Moses, holding his rod up
With those others embracing his hands.
No one said it would be quick,
And I know you may be tired.
Just look up on that cross to see Jesus,
To know that He is a fighter.
She wouldn't of brought you here
If you wasn't strong enough to sustain.

We simply hold our ground,
And continue praying.
By all faith , singing Psalms and Hymns to the Lord.
This warfare is spiritual; Never give up fighting for the Lord.
Against all forces of evil, all the glory be to the creator.
The enemy She already defeated.
Now through this test we must believe.

"Therefore, since we have this ministry, as we have received mercy, we do not lose heart."

2 Corinthians 4:1

My Letter to the Congregation 06-04-2011

Dear Fearless Faith Congregation,
Thank you for all the positive encouragement,
And taking me in, when no one else out there did.
Pastor Cotton, you looked over mine iniquity,
And only treated me as God would.
That home is my true sanctuary!
A real safe haven.
My vision can only see the growth;
The greatness to abound.
During my time away from the temple
I will continue to read, and with God, favor I have found.
Your love and knowledge is molding me
No matter how long they may take me away.
This faith will not drop.
Thank you for providing a safe place,
For the Lord's inspiration.
Never would have known that this Word was in me.
Found the strength to stand up afront the congregation!
The spirit of the Lord works amazing through me.
When we just continue by faith
Knowing that He never promised that
Everyday would be a good day.
We dance through the reign.
And smile past the tears
Finding joy in the heartache
And strength through the disappointing years.
See the mystery in our misiries.
Notice the good tidings along the path.
We notice the destination,
But it's the journey to get there that matters.
We'll all go different ways,
Led by many fates

Just dont forget to tell your testimony to others
Along the way.
This journey is not for you,
But generations following behind you.
Pay attention to the clues.
You may be leaving behind.
They will be important for those following behind.

Do You Know Jesus? 06-05-2011

How many of us can dare to say that we really know Jesus?
The miracles performed, the lives reborn!
Were you called down out of a tree?
The prophetic message that his time was to be.
And from his cup of suffering, that we too would drink.
To pre-speak of his resurrection
Did you rebuke his death?
Concerned with the earthly blessings
When in time there will be nothing of it left.
When He told you to sell all and come back an apostle,
Did you turn and run away?
Mind stayed on your worldly possessions
Not quite wanting to believe in The Way.
When He told you to leave father, mother, sister, brother,
And leave wife and kids to follow me!
Were you willing to go,
Or did He have to first rip away from you everything!
No one having put his hand to the plow,
And looking back is fit for the kingdom of God.
Tell me if you know Jesus!
What was Her conversation with the robbers?
Give me the reasoning, For one shall leave and one shall stay!
How was not a bone broken,
When He hung there on that tree for three days?
Can you find the meaning behind the side piercing?
And the flowing of the blood and water?
If you are the bread of life,
How can your flesh we eat and your blood we swallow?
Why should I fast?
When there's so much around for me to eat or drink?

If you are the Son of God,
Why couldn't you save you, or me?
Why wouldn't God remove you?
You didn't even scream?
Do you know Him carnally or spiritually?
Thank you for going to the Father,
And leaving your helper here to guide me.

The Lost Sheep 06-05-2011

"For the Son of man has come to save that which was lost, what do you think? If a man has a hundred sheep, and one of them goes astray, does He not leave the ninety-nine and go to the mountains to seek the one that is straying? And if She should find it, assuredly, I say to you, She rejoices more over that sheep than over the ninety-nine that did not go astray. even so it is not the will of your Father who is in heaven that one of these little ones should perish."

Matthew 18:11-14

How far will God not go, to find His lost sheep?

"Or what woman, having 10 silver coins, if She loses one coin, does not light a lamp, sweep the house, and search carefully until she finds it? And when she has found it, she calls her friends and neighbors together saying, 'rejoice with me, for I have found the piece which I lost!'"

Luke 15:8

Was not the fatted calf killed when the lost son came home?

"Like wise, I say to you, there is joy in the presence of the Angels of God over one sinner who repents."

Luke 15:10

Keep Straining 06-06-2011

What are you straining with?
Right now as your rowing?
Well remember there's more, in the same boat as you.
Straining against the waves,
Wind pushing you back with every move.
Steadily praying to God
Believing Jesus has forgotten about you.
Well don't ever forget, He summoned you,
Called you into the boat!
Told you to row away.
While you're fighting against the elements,
He is gone into the mountain to pray.
Now when He comes to see your boat
Still in the middle of the sea
Exactly what is it that your countenance will be?
Though He's still on land
From so far away He can still see every wrinkle of your face.
Have you given up?
Or do you still keep the faith?
Now when he comes to you, walking on the sea
Should She pass you bye?
When you see Her walking across the tumultous sea
Will you believe? Or begin to cry?
No, it's not a ghost, She see's you in your trouble.
"Be of good cheer! It is I:Do not be afraid."
Then He touches your boat
And the wind and waves pass away.
Just keep rowing your boat
Gently down the stream
Especially in the midst of the storm.
Hold fast to your belief. Don't be surprised,
When She amazes your hardened heart
Just keep on straining, with all of your heart.

My Debt to Society 06-06-2011

"Ephraim: For God has caused me to be fruitful in the land of my affliction."

Genesis 41 : 52

Taking my time to find God
In order to enter into Her Kingdom.
Reading multiple times about repenting and forgiveness.
Down on my knees, crying in front of the cross,
Looking to find Jesus.
Looking to fix what has been wrought.
Patiently waiting for the spirit to pick me up,
Telling me to take up my bed and walk.
Already knowing I would make mistakes
And that's why my soul He pre-bought.
Like all good things, She was willing to pay it forward
Now by the stripes of Him, My life can be born again:
Volunteering my time for good
And giving material riches away;
Donating money to save schools,
And giving the homeless a place to stay.
Helping family members through college,
By whatever may fit the need.
Being a pillar of strength
For my society!
When no one even knows, this comes through me:
Opening abandonded houses,
Making homes for orphaned kids;
No time to even talk about it
Only brag about what God has did.
With me locked away on Patmos
This obviously couldn't come from me.
First fruits to the church,
Thank you for giving this fresh start onto me.

Now God is using me as the Edgar Allen Poe
Of modern day spiritual poetry.
Shakespeare's to be my talent,
But God control's the hand of me.
Telling me exactly what to say!
I'm simply a mere mortal man.
Thank you for attracting this wealth onto me
In order to help fellow man.
I'm just repaying my debt to society
Leaving God's mark on society,
Before going away to be with the King.

Let Him Be Crucified 06-06-2011

"His blood be on us and our children."

Matthew 27:25

Pilate washed his hands and said,
"I am innocent of the blood of this 'Just person.' You see to it."
How often do we kill?
Just people giving society what it wants?
No time for second chances nor forgiveness
Just another life we attempt to defunct.
This is nothing personal. I'm just doing my job!
John the baptist lost his head,
For the pleasure of king Herod.
Had to keep his word,
And give the daughter what she wants.
The one to proclaim the name of Jesus,
And look how he was lost.
One more of God's soldiers gone, thy will be done.
How many got thrown into prison?
Or into early graves have gone?
Rest in peace Martin Luther King Jr.
Sorry Malcolm that you had to so early rise.
Tupac and Biggie got critically shot
Von Von in my heart you will always reside.
Out to make change in the name of the Lord.
Let them be crucified, taken from the game.
Martyrdom be the name for the way we go up.
Kill me if you dare,
For Rich my prayers continually go up.
Conscience white as snow
Like gladiator in this ring,
Get ready for the show.
All hail to the King!

"I Saw satan Fall Like Lightning From Heaven."

Luke 10:18

"Repent, for the Kingdom of heaven is at hand."

Pharaoh hardened his heart,
And at other times it was hardened by God.
One man prayed, 'Thank you God that I'm not like him!'
The other banged his chest,
And simply said, "Have mercy on me God."
Peter was Jesus's disciple,
And he didn't even ask him to explain.
Called him to the shore and told him to eat.
Now go back to proclaiming in my name.
Whose worshiped Baal?
What graven images might you have on you?
How many have cursed God's name?
Is it better to reign in hell? Or to serve in heaven? Do choose.
How much care have you given to someone else's feet?
Rubbing in between the toes, and Filing the nails.
Who says you're lower than me?
Free to make our own decisions through this hell,
But how many will train themselves?
To heed the voice of Jesus
Carnal desires will flood our minds,
But how many are spiritual enough to make them flee from it?
The deepest fear?
You are more powerful than you know.
Why hide your light under the lampstand?
Let it shine bright for the whole world to know.
Would you sell me your birthright?
If I offer you something to eat?
If I sold you into bondage and slavery,
Could you turn around and forgive me?

Let everything you do be done in love

Corinthians 16:14

Tired of the Rain 06-06-2011

Lost in the wilderness, out in the middle of this storm.
All glory be to God, that I have this here gear to put on:
Rain-boots secured, and rain-coat on.
Umbrella on deck,
And She even gave me these rain pants to put on.
But my countenance has become low!
Waiting for the storm to pass.
I'm tired of dancing alone
Send me some hope, or a Mate to help the time pass.
My heart continues to move forward,
But my mind misses what's behind.
Just to have a hug from my kids,
Or a smile from my wife.
Another sunday in my Fathers house!
Right now what is it worth to me?
To simply be able to walk to the refrigerator,
Or use my own toothpaste to brush my teeth!
God I know you have me on a journey,
But like the Israelites, home is where I want to be.
Turn back around, and take all that has been done away.
This time in the wilderness is so far away from everything.
I Am one who enjoys thunder and lightning,
But this has been going on for 30 days straight.
With no permanent shelter,
I just use what tent that I may.
Thank you God for this lighter
And this lampstand to keep the water away.
Trying to drown me out, but only you can quench my faith!
Like Moses, I can only wait for the clouds,
And know that it is you telling me the correct way.
I'm so tired of the rain.
Hoping the sunshine will break through at any day.

When I can finally pull out my sandals,
And put this rain gear away.
Believing that God knows what He's doing.
I keep the mind stayed on Jesus's way.
Lean not unto thine own understanding
Because we may never know the reason.
One day we're here and the next we're gone.
My God works miracles!
Even in such a barren and desert space as this one.

I Am the Lord's Gangster 06-06-2011

Form your pre-conceived notion of me,
My exterior does not show the heart.
Looks to be deceiving,
You have to know people by their heart.
A good tree cannot bear bad fruit.
A bad tree won't bear good.
Catch me in my royal blue and purple!
Yellow and gold.
My Lord has allotted me this,
Gave me these garments!
As soon as I came back home,
Back to the world.
He is my King, who dresses me in princely clothing.
Call all of the people in the village
And tell them my son has come home.
While I been away I've been doing hits,
And kidnapping in the name of the Lord!
Killing demons aint easy!
Neither is leading them in the correct way.
Stacking grands for His kingdom,
But none of this is blood or drug money we hold.
Believing heavily in my O.G.
Yes God is my Big Homie.
His gang of misfits! All my people!
None of them can claim to be perfect
We all got something ill.
Jesus is the enforcer! Taking our problems away.
With the angels as captains and Lieutanants
By belief we tell trees to wither away.
Teaching the children to do our dirty work;
We send them to school each sunday.

Showing them how to keep the organization alive
When it's their turn to run it.
Falling through the ranks, step by step.
Yeah, you can label me a gangster
And with the power of my Lord,
I'll even make a positive out of that.
Take it how you want,
This gangbanging for Christ is where it's at.

You Have No Power Here 06-07-2011

"Behold, I give you authority to trample on serpents and
scorpions, and over all the power of the enemy, and nothing shall
by any means hurt you."

Luke 10:19

You have no power here!
No authority has been given to you
You're only allowed to do what my Mother O.K.'s you to.
You would have never even been in the Garden of Eden
If my Father didn't make a way.......
Wouldn't have been able to test Job
If my God didn't allow you to have it your way.
Nothing to do with you. Just testing the faith of me.
Seeing if I've been paying attention
To the lessons He's been trying to speak.
When the world went dark. Her children possessed the light;
You have no strength over me, no control over this life.
Legion had to ask
To be allowed to enter the swine,
And it was not until Jesus said.
Before down the hill they could slide,
Into the lake to drown:
No power over my finances;
Loved ones, or family and friends;
Even while I live in your home!
This dweling space you are not allowed in.
I felt you step foot in, while I tried to sleep.
Even in my dreams you found out; God protects me!
Woke up just in time! The Lord wanted me to see you flee.
Given me confirmation
That there is nothing you can do to me!

In times of crisis, even demons call on Gods name.
Bowing to Jesus authority.
Never forget, He has given us of the very same.
Practice using your power, and watch how the devil will fade!
satan I rebuke you. Get you behind The Way.
Send him back to the pits!
Don't be afraid to slap him through the gates
My God gives this power to you and me.
Send him back to the pits where he should stay.
My God gives this power, to you and me.
We are but a bucket from a well!
Come and drink.
My Momma always said, if you dont use it, you lose it;
Don't let your powers fade away.
Don't wait until it's too late.
Start whipping on satan today!
Without even getting in the ring.
This power is available to all by faith,
Including you and me.
It's still there even if you should fall.

"Then He called his twelve disciples together and gave them power
and authority over all demons, and to cure diseases. He sent them
to preach the kingdom of God and to heal the sick."

Luke 9:1-2

God 06-07-2011

"You believe that there is one God. You do well. Even the
demons believe, and tremble."

James 2:19

His faith is so high,
His belief is so huge!
He's given that to Jesus,
And Jesus gives that to me and you.
No they don't work alone.
Having servants that they tell to go and to come.
Some want you to believe, the thought was of many Gods,
But we know there's only Won.
Follow the scriptures, to know that there are many g-o-d's
And that large list of small g's, includes you and me.
She's miraculous!
She's wonderful.
She's the only one.
She's brought meaning to the moon,
And give reason to the son.
Told the waves where to stop.
The only one who knows how far the ocean is deep.
She's way beyond our small mind,
Much farther in the galaxy than we could ever see!
Whenever man thinks he knows something,
He finds out he really knows nothing at all.
God can use the full capacity of the mind
When we only use a small portion of ours.
Pleadies, Orion, who could it be?
Heaven or hell?
Who could in both of these be?
She's mighty,
She's fierce.
Compassionate and caring.

She's just
She's fair
Bold and daring!
My God is all powerful, but only some will see.
Thank you God for giving us this power;
Like how He uses me.

"Ephraim: For God has caused me to be fruitful in the land of my
affliction."

Genesis 41:52

I Am a Great Warrior 06-07-2011

"How beautiful upon the mountains are the feet of him who brings good news, who proclaims peace, who brings glad tidings of good things, who proclaims salvation, who says to Zion, 'Your God reigns!'"

When I close my eyes,
I can see me on the battlefield.
Decided to venture into the enemies camp,
With these chosen few here!
No time for a war speech,
Just see the glory in my eyes!
The general has sent me here;
It's time for this devil to die.
With shield at the ready, and rod in hand,
Muscles bulging and sweating
Knowing I feel God's hands.
Breastplate girded tight
And the word in the loins.
Waiting for the sun to go down
Fully on His terms we going.
Garments of vengeance for clothing, and clad with zeal as cloak.
I feel the troops standing behind! Like geese ready to blow,
On a mission back north; Knowing what we may be facing,
Soon as the facemask on this helmet of salvation comes ablazing.
Like braveheart or gladiator,
I am a warrior, call me Mason!
his troops have ours multiplied and compounded,
But of faith, we have way more than his.
Like Jesus I won't lose any
Coming home with those you gave to me and more.
We don't fight this war for us,
But for those at home with the babes!

Not of the earthly realm, but in the spiritual realm we blaze.
Just look at this platoon
There are plenty of women here in the ranks too!
Ready for battle!
Already having envisioned taking over the enemy camp soon!
We make imagination become realty until it is truly the end.
This is a surprise attack!
The enemy can't win.
Tired of you attacking us!
So we coming for you.
Right in the midst of your home
So your troops will be confused.
We are the 10%,
and the 1% er is me.
Like a sumari warrior
Your whole team must bleed!
Michael stands in front of us,
Ready to lead.
For all the drama you started in heaven
It's gonna be hell to cash in!
Leaving you in chains!
And taking back what belongs to children of the day.
It's time for this war to be finished!
This battle has been going long before time.
When God has us done here,
The son of perdition will come home with mine!

Dear Sister Karolyn,

    Not sure if this will reach you before your surgery, but know that I wrote it right now. After I got your letter and prayed on it.

Declaration of Faith 06-08-2011

Where two or more are gathered in my name,
I am sure to be in the midst of them.
We stand around the congregation,
Giving all of the praise to Him!
Thank you for blessing the doctor with a steady hand,
And allowing him to work by your faith.
Thank you for providing her with so much determination.
The want to see the new day.
Thank you for taking all of our fears and worries!
And allowing us to cast all of our cares on you!
Thank you for your word telling us
That for those who believe, you will come through.
Thank you for walking with her,
And keeping her with you!
While the medical team repairs her tent
You keep her soul safe with you!
Thank you for providing us this faith
Knowing that when it's done She will come to.
Thank you for her speedy recovery,
And allowing her at least one more day,
Before you take her home with you.
With you, a day is as a thousand years,
And a thousand years as a day.
Thank you for continuing her light
To spread optimism to Fearless Faith,

Thank you for the power you have,
"Do not worry she only sleeps."
We believe in your miracles
So this healing is already done through Jesus.

How Many Times 06-08-2011

To forgive and forget,
Or to not forgive at all.
How do I accept an apology?
When I Am the one who has been wronged?
How can I see a sincere apology?
Or measure one's level of remorse?
I would love to forgive you,
But how will that remove the hurt?
Restitution and court fees!
Won't do much for me.
Counseling and psychotherapy;
You hurt me just to watch my heart bleed.
How to just let that go?
Jesus I know what you said,
But this hurt festers deep within my soul.
How do I allow my heart to be free?
What will take this mind to at ease?
Jesus says right now, but I just need a little more time to see.
Some say for me to just force it.
Everyday to speak it through my teeth.
The plan is that,
Eventually my heart will one day believe.
After you cut me through my soul,
How will I just let that pain go?
They tell me I'm the one who's hurt by my own unforgiveness;
This pain tormenting my soul.
Why do I say I forgive you, if the pain still does not go away,
What's the point in forgiving
If either way the hurt will remain?
Millions of little ones?
Or one big one? Which one's worse?
Look at what you did to me!
How will forgiveness take away this hurt?

"Take heed to yourselves. If your brother sins against you, rebuke him; And if he repents, forgive him, and if he sins against you seven times in a day, and seven times in a day returns to you, saying, I repent. You shall forgive him."

Luke 17: 3-4

An Amazing Ride 06-08-2011

When most would only find fear in this journey:
My soul only rises!
Showing me the power we have over evil,
When we only give love a try.
The best way to overcome our fears,
Are simply to face them.
Scared to learn how to swim
Then I threw you into the deep end!
Scared of heights?
Then skydiving will by the hobby for you.
Scared to be confronted by evil!
Then step foot in the devils play room.
My Lord doesn't provide a spirit of fear,
But of power and love, and a sound mind.
Faith is what He's all about.
Scared to lose love?
Then let it go.
If it comes back it's yours to keep,
If not you'll never know.
Scared to live!
Then take an opportunity to die.
Scared to die?
Then decide to take charge and live!
Fear is not for God's children,
Just those he gave over to a debase mind.
But when we live by faith.
Even the worst situations
Turn out to be an amazing ride.

Paul's Thorn 06-09-2011

"And lest I should be exalted above measure by the abundance of the revelations. A thorn in the flesh was given to me, A messenger of satan to buffet me, lest I be exalted above measure."

2 Corinthians 7

Drugs and alcohol! What may it be?
Finances, or maybe even an incurable STD.
Diseases, or a lustful eye?
Maybe a lack of faith.
Cursing and defying God,
Or even working for satan.
Some refuse to forgive
Others won't give what they have.
Some are selfish. And others walk by foolish pride.
When something goes good, on who is it that you boast?
When good goes bad, in whose name do you gloat?
How could I take the good from God and not suffer some
Shame?
Will you be able to stand with He?
Through a little bit of folly and some shame?
For our light affliction, which is but for a moment,
Is working for us a far more exceeding and eternal weight of Glory.
These words don't come from me, just turn to Paul's story.
How many would be bitten by snakes, beaten and shipwrecked,
And dare to move on?
Some of us just receive a splinter! And can't go on.
How steadfast is your dedication?
Or is your faith focused upon your thorn?

"For therefore I take pleasure in infirmities, in reproaches, in needs, in persecutions, in distresses, for Christ's sake. For when I Am weak, then I Am strong.

2 Corinthians 12:10

A positive attitude causes a chain reaction of positive thoughts, events, and outcomes. It is a catalyst and it sparks extraordinary results.

Mastering Law of Attraction

My Angel Of The Lord 06-12-2011

Many people say, "I can't see mine."
I know mine is here with me.
Sent here to minister unto me by the Lord;
I feel it's presence here with me.
Fighting off satan's forces,
And other demonic beings we cant see.
Here on guard like a pitbull,
Watching over me, even while I sleep.
All believers have them!
Ready and willing to lead.
How many of us practice vision from the third eye
With each and every decision we must defend?
Always on Won accord.
And with a simple whistle,
Can instantly summon a thousand more my way.
We like to label things, 'accidents':
A window suddenly opening;
Or the slamming of a door.
Not being familiar with earthly,
How could we ever read the heavenly language that's here
On earth?
The complex simplicity of doves wings
Or eagles floating effortlessly through the storm.
We've been given power in this world,
Ability to summon our ministered angels to attack!
Once you learn to use your power,
May the world stand back.
No matter what our situation here on earth may be.
They are always free!
Readily waiting on the Lords command,
And right back they come to sit at our feet.
But don't listen to me first hand,
Take time through the scriptures to read.

Ask God to open the eyes of the heart Lord
And give you the gift to see.

Kicked Outta Hell   06-09-2011

What happens when you visit satan,
And he realizes the thrill is gone?
Trying with all of his might to conquer you, but realizing
That the war is done.
"Now when the devil had ended every temptation, he departed
from him until an opportune time."

I went into satan's house and came in proclaiming of peace.
When the message wasn't answered,
I just wanted to leave, and shake the dust off of my feet.
Here to do greater work! I was made to stay.
Forced to put up with his seeds,
And guards for more than 30 Days.
With multiple attacks, he tried to subdue me!
All I could do was focus on the hands and feet of the king.
Many of the nights I lay awake,
Meditating! In my mind screaming out Jesus' name.
Everytime they heard it, his demons would run away.
Only they continued to come back, with each passing day.
With my mind stayed on God's word
I prepared for what I might face;
Likening myself to a soldier, that's headed for war.
With the physical eye feeling overpowered,
I had to close my eyes and from the soul see more.
Revert to 2 Kings 6:15 and everything was alright.
With the devil getting no foothold,
Seeing God's power to be too bright.
he again became afraid. Fear of a Son of Light!
As the light began to radiate and overcome his people.
he decided to do what any war torn leader would do.
With my mindset as God's soldier, A prisoner of Christ!
he called the first thing smoking,
And had them give me a ride.

Bushel Basket 06-13-2011

Once upon a time there was a feeble man
Who carried a large, empty, bushel basket.
The bushel basket was so bulky, heavy, and empty!
I will fill my bushel basket he excited!
And took it to the king.
"King. I request of you to fill my bushel basket."
The feeble man triumphed unto the king!
His faith held strong,
Although he could feel his wobbly knees.
"Why would I fill your large bushel basket?" The king roared!
"Your goodness exceeds forever!"
The weak man implored,
"And if you give unto me,
Then I can give unto others all the more."
The king began to rub his chin,
With a grin on his face.
"Leave your bushel basket here, and go your way.
And come to me in the morning, at the break of day."
The weak man slept outside, right beyond the king's gate.
That night he couldn't even sleep.
He just stare up at the stars and pray.
Up with the Son!
Contemplating of all of the good he will do with his goods,
Skipping back to the king.
"There's my gift to you!"
The weak man's basket was fulled over the brim,
Heaping with gifts of all kinds.
So grateful to the king, he could only begin to cry.
The basket was now way too heavy.
How now? Could ever his basket be moved?

Fifty Four 06-18-2011

How many must it take?
Before we can lock the whole world away?
I can count at least 54, just in my state.
Over one-half it's population! All locked away.
So who is failing in this picture?
My county, the city? Country, or State?
No jobs to provide for the people, but the federal government
Will pay to lock us away.
I know they won't like what I'm saying,
But I'll talk anyway.
I've spent some time on the inside,
And all of the fault be accredited onto me.
Now that I'm inside, There is only madness I see.
No thoughts on reformation,
Rehibilation maybe used to be.
Corrections, but no education,
Good thing I already came with my college degree!
There's lots of learning here,
But I label it informal schooling.
Some are taking up shop, and it's a dangerous board they pursuing.
Displaying the toys that are being used here;
Grown men tools!
Many will never know their combinations!
Locks being used for something else.
Problem eliminated.
If we start out in society,
Giving the people a reason to achieve.
Prisons would not be necessary any more
If there were jobs for him and me! We'd all have hope.
$40,000 will buy a top dollar education,
But you pay $80,000 to incarcerate me!
Tell me who calculates this math?

And why audits don't show?
Here lies the red tape in this crime scene?
Fifty four plus prisons!
Compare that to the Michigan schools
That have been ceased.
With our children's dreams getting closed down
Where else do we expect them to stay?
Run to what avails in abundance!
Though you also just cut fire and police pay.
Squeezing the deputies!
Flop all the little fish, and big ones too!
No tickets! But still longer I must stay here with you!
1st time prisoners!
The federal government will pay.
What you focus on, you create more of
Whether negative or positive.
The Michigan crime rate has to stay high!
Do you know how much money is made out of this?

Kill the leaders,
Close the schools.
Black Panthers gone extinct,
SCLC all confused.
NAACP, dont talk to me
Marcus Garvey!
Told to move.
Martin Luther King assignated!
Malcolm X!
Assaignated too!
Nat Turner,
One of the greatest.
Egyptian kingdoms,
Dissimenated.
African continenet,
Flat raped.
Native Americans!
Tricked and hated.
Japanese!
Even played em:
Concentration camps;
Relocate em.
Robbing and stealing;
Is what made US.
Now justice!
Is so over inflated
That even children
Catching cases.
What's the growth?
For this nation?
Independence!

Our motivation.
The more we earning,
The more they taking.
Value Failing.
To other nations.
Drugs and alcohol;
People complacent
Clear your mind,
And see what we facing.
The true battle,
Lies with
En-A Me,
The battles within
Just see the truth
And we can win.
Money motivated,
But with you I'll split.
Material resources!
Only important to him.
There's more than enough
That we can live.
By God we blessed
Not luck or Whim
But planning braced it.
What's next?
After this?

Praise the Lord 06-16-2011

"Praise the Lord, all you gentiles! Laud him, all you peoples! For his merciful kindness is great toward us, and the truth of the Lord endures forever."

Psalm 117

So many people in today's world say, "I'll pray for ya!"
Well I don't want you to pray for me!
Pray to God only for the initial manifestation,
But only praise him after that for me.
Praise God for me like you're prayer has already been answered!
Now how many will just believe?
I speak to you from the voice of a believer!
So there won't be many who'll agree.
My Jesus told us to speak those things that be not
As though they were!
If you must, then open up and re-read.
All things are possible,
But only according to your level of belief.
Look at that mountaintop!
The fig tree.
Then compare that to a mustard seed.
All according to your level of faith and belief!
Praise the Lord!
He will come back looking for that church
Whose voice can be heard screaming His name out of it's doors.
Praise the Lord continually from night to day.
Read the 5th division of Psalm's, there is no other way.
How many of us pray amiss?
Continually asking for the same thing.
Give it to God just one time.
Then praise until it comes.

"Praise God in his sanctuary; Praise him in his mighty firmament! Praise him for his mighty acts; Praise him according to his excellent greatness! Praise him with the sound of the trumpet; Praise him with the lute and harp! Praise him with the timbrel and dance; praise him with stringed instruments and flutes! Praise him with loud cymbals; Praise him with clashing cymbals! Let everything that has breath praise the Lord. Praise the Lord!"

Psalm 150

So Close To God 06-12-2011

The birds and clouds dwell in the first heaven.
Second entertains the galaxies and stars.
Who's ever seen the third heaven?
Not even spaceships,
With high powered lenses from afar.
With the earth as God's footstool,
And how lowly is me?
How is it that my earthly form?
Can be constantly in the presence of the King?
Much smaller than my eyes to an ant
When He looks down upon me!
Yet the hairs on my head He has counted,
My heart and mind She already can see.
Such a microscopic operation for Her,
To take the soul right up and out of me.
Liver, pancreas, to DNA
How did His large fingers ever fit into such a little space?
Like looking into an atom without a microscope
Is His eyesight on me.
Yet I Am always in His presence,
However could this be?
The infinite wonders of His majesty
My finite mind will never understand
Do all the planning that I want!
Still I could not come up with a tenth of His plan.
How could I control this life?
It's better to just let it be.
Hand over the control panel to Her spirit,
In the presence of God is the only place I long to be.

The Elite Unit 06-19-2011

Who could ever join a team?
That didn't train it's soldiers to win?
Women! On a battlefield, we are ready for war.
Tore! Through your whole team, before the ref even said go.
Slow! To be your reflexes, because you failed to train like this.
Kiss! Face in the dirt, when you messing with grown ass men.
Win! Is all we know how to do.
Two! Is all we need for this, but bring your whole platoon.
Mushroom! Like a cloud of smoke,
When the US dropped the Oklahoma bomb!
Atop. Is where we stand, when all of the smoke is gone.
Tears! Is what your general shed.
I know, we've been doing this for too long.
Fear! Turns out to be motivation for those with me.
Dumb. Is how the others get left,
When they find out how quickly we proceed.
True! To the brotherhood, not the normal fraternity.
We facing, tough times, no it aint about gang banging.
Done slanging, now that we can get it legit.
Split, the profit with the whole community. Not all about selfish
Uplift this! So we move it all together now.
Frowns! Is what we in the business of turning upside down.
Mounds. The amount of cash we got on hand
Land. Planes in foreign lands!
Fate! Is all ours when we move with the Lords mighty way,
Plan. To achieve more and in the most positive way
Stay. Learning this literature until my dying day.
Pay. Is all we make, but it aint about the dough
Poe. Is what my family used to be, but we aint no moe.

What's The Reason? 06-12-2011

I've done military training,
And prison is where I currently be.
After living on both sides,
I notice they both have some striking similarities:
Who goes to chow;
Cleans their racks;
Puts on a uniform when they go out,
And BDU's when they get back?
Questions must filter through the ranks
When my problem is right here and now.
Time in isolation, away from the world in the here and now.
Being stripped of humanistic characteristics.
Brainwashed and trained to defer,
Who wants to stand down?
When my Lord instructs me to rise up!
I'm not afraid to look you in the eye
My God gives this authority to us.
How and when to sleep,
This is just wayyy too much.
The one that it's taken from, or he who doesn't truly have it;
Where's freedom!
A paycheck, or the unlimited earnings potential we receiving?
Is what the Lord gives unto me.
From behind these bars,
I'll make more than in your lifetime, you'll ever see.
Why are these two so related?
I've yet to find out.
But they each give me the same feeling;
Waiting for the angels of my Lord
To come and break me out.

Some things are just not meant to be understood,
Just the American way.
Some find strength in having the law behind its authority
Some see pride in going the correct way.
I stand on the governing line, fully committed to neither way!
My only want is to save both side;
I'm going to be a preacher.
Using myself to light the way!
Message to all that it reaches.
Near, or far and away!
Left here to teach a mission
Knowing that the path is created by my each passing day.
That others will one day take.

God is the benefactor.
All glory be to the king!
We consistently doing push-ups and sit-ups.
Digging the dirt up around this tree.
Re-fertilize it's root's.
In hopes that it will produce!
If no fruit grows with the next harvest,
You know exactly what we must do.
He is the vine! And simply a branch is me.
How can He pull one out,
And graft anew right back where one used to be?
I believe in miracles!
So lets turn this water into wine.
The disciples were only halfway there,
Though they paddled all night.
With just a touch of the finger,
He landed them safely onto the shore!
Who else could perform such miracles?
None other than my Lord!

All In The Family 06-22-2011

Whose fault could it be? That we both ended up in here?
I trusted in you, and you trusted in outside peers.
Took a gamble on life and lost out on those we love.
Both of us got daughters out there, growing up in the world.
We were supposed to guide them.
How do we do that from in here?
I know I knew better.
Let evil thoughts seep into the ear.
To live and to learn.
Repent and run the other way.
Right into my Fathers arms,
He'll come and get us, if we can just make it half way.
Put us back into his kingdom!
Won't even ask what happened.
He's an on time God,
Who speacilizes in human grafting.
He may not come when we want Him,
But He'll be there right on time.
It's critical to give Him all faith;
To put no belief in mine.
It's all love till our dying day
Your blood will always be mine,
But never again will I be pulled away.
Before,
During,
Or
After
I finish doing this time.

You have to have confidence in your vision or else no one else
will trust in it

Mary Katrantzou

Rage 06-21-2011

How many have fury with this system?
Wondering where does the injustice end?
Supposedly all were brought from vietnam
So why does the story come into play again?
Can't find Osama, but we can find a penny under the sea.
Tell me slavery is dead!
How many niggers have these C.O.'s called me!
If I come up lost in prison,
Then I guess, to the world I've revealed too much.
Martin Luther King dissapeared,
Then malcolm X was immediately next.
Say what you want to,
But the Nation of Islam didn't sleep him.
While we telling the truth
By whom were those pamphlets about the Black Panthers
Truly written?
Covering up your follies!
Is what the U.S. is known to do.
North against South!
For human labor, your brother had war with you!
In here I work all day, but you keep all of the pay.
How many times is the Federal government willing to cash out?
In order to ensure my stay?
How many were found guilty? Just because of their race?
The green mile was not a fairy tale.
Whose mind could dream up that place?
So many know the truth,
But like Watergate look the other way.
My country was created in wrongdoings
How much of Able's blood must bubble away?
My Lord does take account of how many graves,
The ocean has swallowed up to date.

An American passage! Trace back high blood pressure
Now tell me slavery was so far away.
It's effects are still here, blatantly on the inside of me.
No Crips and Bloods, but it's time to unite!
Vice Lord and G.D.'s lets get together and do this right.
satan has divided forces, but it's not too late.
Latin Kings! Mexican Mafia.
This whole world we will overtake.
Together on a unified mission
No bitching no more.
They love to see us all kiling each other,
Or to end up behind locked doors.
Coroporate exec's sit back and watch the funds roll in.
Nothing going on in here is worth
What the tax payer's dollars spend.
Yes, I'm angry!
This slave ship is a ghost.
Riding off of the backs of the ones who built it before.
No education and no money for jobs
Of course the situation is discouraging.
Folks are getting robbed, while you make 500k a year;
Mom and dad cant get a job to feed the kids.
And there was another school shooting again.
How much is too much?
And what is necessary to get by?
To overthrow this human built, unjust machine,
Is the only goal of mine.
How to use this anger for fuel?
To Appropriate positive new beginnings!
By my rage I'd like to explode,
Rather find a positive way to pursue in this.

I'm heartbroke 06-22-2011

Who's going to be there for her,
Now that daddy aint home?
To shelter and encourage her,
Keeping her far from harm.
Kindergarten and training wheels!
I know I missed it all.
Should have been there laying your foundation,
Now I can only call.
Hoping letters will keep us close,
I made a deadly mistake.
Taking a chance and thinking
I could make it all even better, more than O.K.
Now I've thrown you away.
With plans to keep you by my side for life.
What Am I to do now?
Stepped down from my career,
Child, step child, and wife!
Now we must all rebuild.
Whatever that may mean.
Just know that I'm heartbroke, and will always love you,
Daddy's little dream!
I will always miss you.
You will always be my world
The reason why I continue to move.
I Am heartbroke.
You will always be daddies lil girl.

Creation of Life 06-24-2011

My energy! Your energy!
What is it that our words will speak?
First there was all darkness,
And then out of that came me.
Conception and birth pains.
From my mother, I was delivered by my Father's words.
Everything your minds speak to being
Cums to life!
Like a verb;
Positive or negative? What type of letters will you write?
Even the knowledge you take in
Will fill your soul with darkness,
Or with light.
With the power of the mind,
Each second our thoughts are creating new things.
It takes a concentrated effort
To be certain that you're creating the correct things.
If I Am in the likeness of He
Then what does that say about me?
The earth was void until understanding was allowed to be.
Now I have that same power, but greater!
Because you have gone back to be with the king.
Universal will be my understanding,
Once I come to terms with the fact;
The universe resides within me.
I Am creation!
My mind orchestrates how and what comes back.
Positive has to be my motivation
If the urge is to build the things right.
This situation brought me down,
But never will it take out my light.

Humble Me 06-23-2011

Lord mine iniquities are great
I counted myself above you.
Not acknowledging myself as the student, but teacher.
Not servant, but master above you!
Knock my soul down!
So I know that there is nothing done without you.
It's easy to be great,
But who wants to work a job that you feel is beneath you?
For Him to increase, I must decrease!
All selfish intent must cease.
All of the praise be to the Lord
None of this success has anything to do with me.
Locked so far away, so that we know that this is all about you.
I earn $2 dollars a day!
While at the same time, Lord what you are able to do!
Cause me to increase, in the land of my affliction!
Could you guess that I'm a billionaire!
If you came to visit me in prison?
My Father allotted me His inheritance,
All of the glory is to She.
Material wealth is not even important for me
I only want to live my life under She.
Live my life till others can't help
But witness His glory all through me.
I'm simply a character in Her book;
This is all His-story:
Producer; Director; And writer. All controlled by He.
I continually praise Him
That She gave me this call.
Not even the main one,
But a simple character in this plot
To others this part would be insignificant

But I know there's a reason He put it in here for me.
I play the part well, with no moaning or complaining.
Simply a service to my Lord
All a part of His greater works for me.

The Pulse of The yard 06-23-2011

Groups here, clutters there, what's really going on:
Chess in a mass; A rapping conglomeration;
Others singing prison songs.
Laughing and talking, what more is there to use for motivation?
Who is out to be the tough ones?
Claiming you, but forgetting about me.
Long time? Or short time? Just a matter of perception to me.
Someone didn't deliver right
So it's time that he be taught a lesson by the Kings.
Phone calls to the outside, just to see what's happening in brief:
"I know it's been 12 years, but in 8 more I'll be free."
From old neighborhoods to new beefs
All things that continue to go on, even without me.
Some leave for visitation,
While others' have had no visit since 1983!
Young and old, or fresh and new.
We find it all together
Pumping through these compounds like vital glue.
Each separate unit coming together to form one unit.
Intertwined by the veins that we call authority.
What is to be seen on the outside is not necessarily
What lies beneath.
Just keep out a watchful eye,
And an ear out to the street.
Listen to the movement until with it you become Won.
Mental visualization;
An uncanny ability to feel what is to come.
What's the ailment for the cancerous cells?
And how do the strong continue to move on?
The strength and the might that must come
When numbers are gone.

Exponential multiplication all in the blinking of an eye.
Taking the time out to analyze
All of the different types that go by.
Living within this system of a breathing organism
Wondering which part is me.
Although this is not the body I would rather live in
It's the system that was appointed onto me.
Now to make the best of this world, is the only key.
On a quest to unlock these doors
Praying for the day when this body
Is no longer the definition of me.

The Kingdom is Within 06-26-2011

How will I externally find joy?
If inside I didn't know what I'm searching for?
Cars, a new home, money in the bank, A corvette from 2024!
What exactly is it that can bring happyness to me?
I'm looking to build me a kingdom,
Yet afraid to take the time to study the King;
That already resides deep down within.
Meditation? or yoga? What can help my syndrome?
Internally I have a complex,
And I'm not exactly sure what is going on.
Apprehensive about the way the world looks at me
When the whole time the issue lies in the way that I see me.
Measuring my self-steem by my net worth will never work for me.
Mental power is the only self knowledge that will truly work.
Take the time to bind satan, and find joy in the imperfections.
The things that make us truly beautiful, are our imperfections.
The creator methodically put you here!
Just the way you are!
What you may label as an imperfection
God has given you for power.
Take the time to learn your heart
To see what really makes you smile;
Bring more of that goodness into your life,
And do away with what brings you plight.
How many are searching for the kingdom?
But refuse to look inside!
Even when the Lord brings joy in life
You still choose to harden the eye.
Love is all we need, and true love lies within.
The heart is well protected,
And only God knows what lies deep down within.
Why do we search and scramble about?

For what already lies within?
How many go through life unhappily
When Peter tells us to find the joy in this.
Mourning is but for a night.
Joy comes in the morning.
My Lord is the creator of light
How could they steal the joy She has put into us?

To See Myself Clearly 06-29-2011

The inside or the outside?
What governs the spirit of me?
How Am I to see myself?
Through the eyes of G-o-d?
Or the way the world sees me to be?
Even looking into the mirror,
I can only see distorted faces:
Cloudy and all marked up; Smudges won't go away,
No matter how hard we try to erase them. Here all the more.
What's this mind game that won't allow me to see me as I Am?
Wanting me to believe that I Am lower than,
Not to see the kingdom that lies within me.
Compare me to an animal and bottle up all of my rage.
No matter what you try to do to me,
I'll still continue living on by faith.
The exterior glows!
Which makes me intriguing to you.
Causing your lifestyle to change
I notice you comparing me unto you.
Wondering where my joy stems from
Why God gives this power to me.
I know you expect me to be lower than,
But never could you look down upon me.
So many are lost, but I refuse to be that one.
Humbling myself unto the Lord
This aint prison!
Too many are only in lost space having fun.
Just money to my state
Because it has a hard time getting it any other way.
Who do I see when I look in the mirror?
Not a prisoner,
But an asset to this state.

All For The Glory 06-26-2011

When bad things happen, for people who do so much good.
For better or for worse,
And then pulled apart by the ways of the world!
Death of the innocence,
A war that should have already been won.
Slipping away from unity,
The stray bullet from an untrained gun!
Why did daddy leave? And how long must he be gone?
Some got shipped overseas,
And many may never be coming back home.
Sickness and disease;
The inner workings of mental health.
To count it all joy! Mind focused on how Jesus left.
To sit with him and the King
I will have to face the same thing.
Endurance is the key,
Won't even ask you to take this suffering away from me.
Only pray for others!
In all hopes that they find the way.
This pain is temporary! My heartache will fade away.
Five years is minimal, Some have multiple natural lives!
How could I complain about my situation?
Crying because I lost my kids and wife.
I will see them again.
Even if as a family we will never be,
I will never turn my back.
Walking together on that stairway to heaven.
God never promised it would be pretty,
As a matter of fact, many of the biblical days were ugly.
Through all of the difficulities we face,
To God must be all of the glory

A New Way to Eat 06-20-2011

No more drugs, or selling dope!
Armed robbery aint the thing for me.
I'm out to show yall
That it is always a new positive way to eat.
Take what I used to do,
But I still wanted more.
Keep planning in this five year stretch.
All about getting some more.
Strength in every way possible:
Mind; Body; and Soul.
But it aint all about me
I want to see you make some goals.
Money aint important
I stake the initial investment!
This is all about bettering people;
Human capital investments.
From writers to illustrators what do you love to do?
Stock investments, transferring capital,
Take the time out to sit down and learn to know you!
Real estate to car sales do you and not me.
Automechanic? Or Engineer? What do you dream to be?
Sit down and put in the work!
Mental fortitude is the key.
Maybe you want to start a church; Get your clergy degree!
A youth center for the kids,
Then take the time out to figure out what you will need.
Brotherhood and unity!
Peace is what we will need.
It's time that we pick our people up,
So that we can all learn a new way to eat.
This is all about the upliftment of communities,
Nothing at all to do with me.

No color to the nutritional gain.
Race isn't a reason to fail.
My Father's provided all of this bread for all.
I'm only to pray for it, drink it, and give it back to all.
Watch the little, as like yeast, it rises to alot
Unbreakable faith in my Lord is all I got.

My Heart Belongs 06-26-2011

Carrying your own cross to calvary,
While beaten half to death.
The pain of your torture is well beyond me,
Thank goodness Simeon was there, to provide you some rest!
Blood trickling into your eyes. You are hoisted onto the cross
With no food and no water! Who else could bear that cross?
Never said a mumbling word!
Just simply kept the faith.
Knowing the scripture must be fulfilled;
For man's fate!
Pierced in the side, until the blood and water seeped away.
Bonded us into God's covenant, and many of us still
Don't understand what the covering of your blood is to say.
Though my sins be scarlet like crimson
You make them as white as snow.
If it were not for God's plan,
Then how would we be able to
Find our place in heaven,
That's already been foretold?
This heart is not mine, although it's situated in my chest
I will hold on to this sacred covenant,
Until you tell me what to do next.
Patiently I wait!
Until you incline to hear my cry.
Bringing me out of this horrible pit, this miry clay,
Setting my feet upon a rock.
Now all I do is praise your name everyday.
Thank you for this brand new song I got.
You put this into my heart.
These new words unto the lord
Thank you for creating this new spark.

If I would have never turned and repented,
Or ran back to the house of my lord!
I'd still be feeding with the swine,
Desiring only the husks of the corn.
You have delivered me from all uncleannesses
Not for my sake , but yours.
All the glory be to you.
For doing through me what I could have never done before.

When we face the worst that can happen in any situation, we grow. When circumstances are at their worst we can find our best.

Elisabeth Kubler-Ross

Wasting My Time 06-27-2011

Got so much to do, that I got no time to waste
This life is all about production,
Even when we can only see the waste.
For the glory of my lord, He can use me at all times
We find so many reasons not to;
When there is a will there is a way to climb.
Some tell me that I dream too big,
But it's God that won't let my faith fade away.
All power be to the mighty Allah!
Find glory in the Almighty just for today.
You believe that I came here alone?
But look at all of God's people standing behind.
Some label me as a pillar,
But only by modesty can this thing be climbed.
Thank you God for lowering me,
And using your might to pull me back up.
Saved me from myself
So I can glorify your name to the world when this is done.
They tell me life is all about patience,
But look how fast paper can burn.
Desires driven by our fires.
The belief in their ability to yearn!
How many have an urging desire?
Now what are you willing to do in order to make it come to be?
Wasting all of my time away
When tomorrow aint promised to be.
Practicing living this life as the last second.
Tomorrow aint promised to we!
I die daily
No matter in what form that death may be.
This life is but for a second;
A speeding ducati, maxing down the street.

You planned for this to hurt me,
But this time away will only sharpen me.
Make the mind and body stronger;
In alliance with the spirirt that God has given to me.
There is no time to waste. The time we live is dead.
Mine is the God of the living
Nothing She instructs me to do is for the d-e-a-d.

Your Number   06-29-2011

I Am somebody!
Not a nobody,
"WHAT'S YOUR NUMBER?"
I Am a human with a name.
"WHAT'S YOUR NUMBER?"
Does me being in prison give you the ability to turn
Your nose up and look down upon me?
"WHAT'S YOUR NUMBER?"
You here with an even longer sentence,
Doing even more time than me.
"WHAT'S YOUR NUMBER?"
Could you be intimidated by my strength and confidence?
The way that God exudes from me?
"WHAT'S YOUR NUMBER?"
You are my sister. United in Christ
So lost chasing a dollar that satan got you afraid to even smile.
"WHAT'S YOUR NUMBER?"
These six digits you give can't capture me!
"WHAT'S YOUR NUMBER?"
It's alright you can be funny but,
Your insecurity with yourself will never penetrate me.
"WHAT'S YOUR NUMBER?"

This Duality That is Me 07-08-2011

Know me as The Great Father;
With a prison number on the back of me.
The great husband,
Who admitted to commiting adultry.
The professor;
Void of understanding.
The state police officer;
Now with a felony!
The lawyer;
That never practiced!
The best friend
That has no one.
The university educated prisoner;
The sheep amongst the wolves!
The free man that's held captive.
A great man misunderstood.
The beast holding on to the prince!
The son of my Father!
The saint,
The liar,
The sinner.
Who will dare to ever even read this?
Why do I even bother?

Straight Aggressively 07-06-2011

Big Brother Kilpatrick!
This shot out is for you.
No matter what this world may say,
We will make it through.
No matter how it happens,
The nigger hunters would love to have our heads.
Mounted up on their walls,
They'll see that they're in for a real positive ordeal;
We will stand tall!
It's hard to imagine
How many of our own people will kick us while we're down.
Then by resilliance when we stand back up,
The world wants to come back around.
Our God is too great!
We will never sit down.
To stand back up is the only way,
And all the glory will be to the crown.
Who holds the crown?
We are here to be beacons,
Inspirations to the world, to turn our negatives into benefits.
Inspire our young boys and girls
With cities and states going belly up
What more are they to do?
Can't let their own people get caught up
So they shift the spotlight onto me and you!
How could we ever sit back,
And like smoke, let this world our character consume?
That's been done too many times before
To so many of our greats.
Now that they can't hang us up,
They have to lock us away.
Using the media to kill our character,

Well that old man has passed away!
Thank you for this new one that's been birthed,
See the God in my faith.
This time in isolation is symbolic for us;
When Jesus hung on that tree for days.
Encaptured by darkness,
Until he was birthed by eternal light.
And he went through it all for a reason!
Endured until he made it to light,
To his Fathers right.
Many failed to believe
That he was sent by the king.
A story so familiar,
To the likeness of you and me!
There is a core group for us
That will never turn away.
Just continue to journey forward with us
Even through our darkest of days.
Big Brother Kwame!
I believe in you, like you believe in me.
I guarantee that we will get back
Simply by doing God's work.
With each new passing day that we see.

Fighting The Invisible 07-06-2011

How do you mount an attack
To fight back against an enemy that you can't even see?
Stand in the middle and fling wildly?
While my enemy sits back and mocks at me?
How can one use the other senses
To turn the tides pointing towards me?
Can I smell the trail of the enemy?
Hear its footprints while I patiently be?
Will I use the vibrations and time the perfect strike
To the perfect place?
When it is that the physical eye cannot even see,
How will I learn to use the third eye by faith?
To mount a finishing attack?
Knowing the fight is never over
We can only battle until the war is won; Loyal soldiers.
This fight is with an unseen enemy
So how do we train for what is to come?
Catch me in the dark room
Training my ears to distinguish
Sounds of the most minute.
Find me in a smell filled room
Training my nose to distinguish and make sense of multiple smells.
Know me in this cramped space meditating
Learning how to stand still.
The enemy has fled now
But at an opportune time he will try me again;
Today, tomorrow, or in 1,000 years!
Not quite sure when he'll try me again.
I focus my mind on his smell,
Replay the sound of his voice in my brain
Feeling the sound of the steps he takes

Remembering how long before each foot places
Pressure upon the floor!
Thank you God for this ability
Instilling in me this want to only win.
Mind stayed on Jesus
Prepared for when he attacks again.

Tip toing until I fell on the wrong side of the line.
When it was all going good, you all stood behind.
Bailed way before impact!
Much before I could have ever given up!
Tossed many resources during this fall;
I couldn't let them all get burned up.
Safely deployed! To land harmlessly on the ground.
My ship is picking up speed, fire raging behind,
Going straight down.
Many ask why won't I just deploy,
But I'm glued into this seat
Must suffer the consequences, for this evil that is me.
Thanks to all that bailed
Many to Jesus did the same.
Will never forget those that stayed down
For those, Jesus came back from the depths of hell!
This world loves to ride when your going up,
And spits upon you on the way down.
Loyalty in this American world, is hardly ever found.
Will die for many things!
Sorry that one of those is not you.
One jumped in with me before impact!
How much more will my Father bless you?
Material is of no importance
This will all be gone one day.
Look to my father and his heavenly kingdom.
As the only way.

To Stand Up 07-16-2011

Push ups and sit ups.
Running the excess fat away.
Bear crawls and burpees
It's my stamina that I want to maintain.
When the squats seem to be too much
And the body refuses to push back against the wait.
With my mind screaming, "That's not enough."
Just one more set
Before you walk away!
With none other for motivation.
Simply me, Jesus and the Holy Spirit.
With the physical ready to give up.
When this tent begins trembling with heavy breathing!
So many others are slumped over,
Or laying prostrate on the ground.
This mind set is to stand up
No matter how bad the pain wants to tear me down.
I can feel it in my ankles, knees, and even my spleen!
The inner me is being renewed,
With each second that the outer me is perishing.
It's not easy to kill him away;
Always trying to come back to life!
No matter how dry the mouth may get!
How shakey the muscles are now.
When you just want to lay down and cry for doubt!
The best thing to do is just stand up;
Straighten the shoulders, and erect the spine!
Choose to stand up.

Walking With satan 07-12-2011

How many of us can say that we walked with satan?
Listened as he gave his spleel to you!
Talked of all the riches that he could bring,
Things that he would give to you!
If you would only go against you.
Shed a little blood to become a part of the family
Maybe just bring a little harm unto the innocent,
Just a lil something to prove that you're worthy
To be a part of his Family.
Being locked away in his house,
Do you decide to play by his rules?
Knowing that his workers stand all around watching,
Waiting to try and bring harm unto you.
Wanting you to just bow down
Because you are so filled with Light.
Though you stand strong and look at him,
Right in the eye.
You must admit, that inside there is some freight.
Stand up for what you believe in?
Or to take the easy way out!
Jesus said I did not come here to bring peace, but division.
But are you really up for this?
Maybe he'll just go away!
Maybe he'll just come on even harder.
But right here and right now I must listen to my heart on this.
To follow my Father, knowing that it may cause my physical to die.
To only stand firm for what I believe in!
Jesus died.
And he never said a mumbling word.
How did I even make it into these miry pits?
Mingling with the scum of the universe
In a highly oppressive and violent place as this.

An open pit of demonic workers,
While angelic is me.
Telling me to commit all of the crime I can
Before I get back to the street.
I took a vow with the lord, long before I ever entered this house.
Now I do stand up strong.
Are you a man or a mouse?
What you may see as weak
When my perception is seeing strength.
Trying your hardest to wear me down,
But the God in me remains my best friend.

To Stand Alone 07-12-2011

How hard is it to stand alone when everyone around you
Is all cliqued up?
They can see the power that resides within
So what you got everyone wants.
Being talked to here and there
Listening to all of the campaigns,
But when all of the talking is done
How will we walk alone again?
Some threaten by physical violence!
How will I come to you after bodily harm!
Some persuade with grown men toys,
Which is not a game in which I'm trying to belong.
Others are so knowledgeable,
But in reality saying the same ole thing.
I came here with street knowledge,
Though almost everything I had is gone;
The world can't take my university knowledge away.
Just know that I'm not stupid!
Nor am I a punk.
But to stand up and fight
Must be for something ones willing to Take a stand!
Nothing here is for me
Just here to serve my time and get home again.
Simply a visitor passing through this foreign land,
This house is not mine.
If you think I stand alone, I suggest
You close your eyes!
See all of these who stand at my side.
Go ahead and pierce my side.
Beat me if you want to,
But I'll never touch the ground.
Though I can take on all of you

I'll decrease to see my God rise.
Still proclaiming of peace!
With no desire to tell on you.
Knowing exactly who you are
Find me back out tomorrow
Lifting weights and doing bear crawls!
I aint never scared!
Some even call me stupid
My God made me built this tough
And to no one do I have to prove it.
Call me an outcast,
Go ahead and shew me away
I'll stand alone, and on my own,
Jesus went the same way.

The Band Plays On 07-16-2011

The beautiful melody of a symphony,
Orchestra or a rock band!
What good would the bang of the drums be?
Without the acoustics of the guitar playing?
How would we ever notice the piano's sweet melody
Without the saxaphone playing beside?
Who could appreciate the beautiful voice,
If no one had tempered the mic?
It would be hard to notice all of those special effects
If the stage crew was not standing by.
Each function maintains its importance in the overall
Production. Even when we can't understand the how or why.
To know my role and fill it.
Not worring about the others;
Who will sing and who will Bam?
When my job is to be out here to serve others.
Who will create light? And when to unleash the smoke?
When my job is simply to open up; To start the show!
Trusting that you know the part
And believing that I will do mine.
Some of us have to stand back,
While others go out to the forefront and shine!
Martha was distracted with much serving,
And Mary sat at Jesus' feet.
Are you the one that is troubled?
Or the one that knows the one thing that is needed?

Made it Through Today 07-19-2011

Some say this separation is a long period of time.
Well it's good that we're no longer focused on distance:
Just to keep the feet moving right along.
Step by step, just to continue running the race!
Now that we've already been entered in it,
We can only choose to put one foot in front of the other,
And keep going on in this way.
Some get distracted by what they could be doing
We only focus on the joy to cum when this is all over.
Even though I run over here,
And you travel in a different place!
Our souls are still locked on the same objective;
Successfully finishing this race!
We run like there is no tomorrow
With no looking back.
Just made it through today!
And tomorrow we'll deal with that.
The most difficult aspect is to get the ball rolling.
Once momentum takes over,
The mass alone will keep this thing going.
Who said this race would be easy?
As long as we get to where it is that we're intended to be.
Just made it through today,
And your love is what keeps me believing.

One day, if you have a little bit of talent and a lot of hard work, you're going to find out who you are

Massimo Bottura

Cutting a Hole in The Net 07-29-2011

"Even so we, when we were children, were in bondage under the
elements of the world."

Galatians 4:3

The wheat shall grow with the tares.
Good shall be enclosed with evil.
The fisherman hopes to find me in the bottom of his net,
But first he has to pull me in from the deep end:
Up from the deep; Bottom of this sea.
Got me snared within this net
With so much garbage atop of me.
Wish I had a knife,
Or that my teeth could chew through these wires.
The heavier with junk this net continues to get,
As the fisherman pulls it up higher.
Will I ever be free of this?
This habitation is not of me.
How did I end up at the bottom of this pit,
When the top I envisioned was for me?
No, I'm not the only one.
Looking around I see plenty of more.
Eyes fixed to the sky, praying for the light to open this dark door.
The higher we climb, the better my eyes can see.
Hoping for that light to be close
When again I can finally breathe.
Closer and closer, he draws us to his yacht;
I can almost hear their laughter, gloating up top,
As He chuckles about the catch he's got.
Not sure of what he may find inside,
But he knows that the net is heavy.
Delegating the catch; Advising His workers to keep it steady!

How could one be so close to His greatness
Yet only wishing for a way out?
So tired that one can barely praise
Too focused on when the suffering will stop.

Do You Believe? 08-05-2011

What's the need to continue fasting?
If the prayer will never be answered
Is the belief
Why continue to eat fruits and vegetables
If the cancer did not get cured when I stopped eating meat?
Why continue to believe in this work?
If it's not even enough to clear the utilities and rent!
Haven't even bought nothing to eat yet
And all of the money has long been spent.
Did all that I was told to do,
But rather than a reduction,
Seen an increase in my time.
Told that mountain to move!
Only thing that happened was that sea went dry.
From marriage to divorce
Where does my strength begin?
Not another obituary from the world
How long have I been locked inside of this pen?
Those that used to send letters!
Don't even write no more.
Those that used to come for visits,
Their faces I no longer even know!
Who once sent me money?
Now my stomach is eating my ribs!
Calls go unanswered,
Without even a letter from my kids!
With this pain in my back and ribs
And my prayer seeming to make it worse!
Who is there to help me of my unbelief
And reveal my blessing in the midst of such hurt?

Search Through The Scriptures 08-11-2011

My heart and mind has a question,
That physically, the answer I can not seem to find.
My spirit asks, seeks, and knocks
Hoping that my soul to find.
Divine intervention!
Is what I need right now.
Help me out of this dilema
Remove the wrinkle from above my brow!
How to know what is reality!
Or what is adopted tradition.
Alot of this just don't add up;
From this book, some pages could be missing.
How do I find what I Am looking for?
When I Am not exactly sure what it is?
Seeing these visions in my dreams
Just couldn't bring back
What these writings on the wall represent.
Why aren't these pictures in my bible?
What does these symbols really mean?
Pray for my soul to remember
Because I forget most of my dreams.
My physical continues the searches
Trying to connect with my spiritual being.
The soul to be the umbilical cord,
How my God unites these worldly things?
What is the meaning of my being?
I just want to know more.
You are the reason for my being
So much more for me to explore!
How am I to grasp understanding
And make wisdom my next of kin?
Give all the earthly away;
I'm calling out to the kingdom that lives within!

Till He Returns 08-11-2011

Day by day I fix my gaze toward the sky.
Patiently waiting, as these years fly on bye
Not yet have I witnessed the angels
But my belief will not let me forget.
What His word says will happen from above!;
Cautiously I listen for the trumpets to begin,
Knowing that this earth will one day pass away.
Isolated from my family and friends,
His return keeps me looking forward to the new day.
Before I go to sleep at each night's end
I speak to Him as if this is the last day before I go home to Him.
Knowing that there is no other way,
I put all of my trust in Him.
Noticing the subtle hints of this world:
Sitting down on a bench to take a drink;
I look in the trees directly overhead to see the doves,
And immediately my thought turns to the King;
My soul is filled with love.
As the doves ascend, I take notice of the reverse order.
Placing all faith in God's plan.
Because only He knows what is in store for us!
I worship only you God.
Jesus you are my blood brother.
At times I imagine the day when you come back to bottle us;
Thank you for opening that door for us.
I love you Lord!
More than I could love any other
Praise God for taking care of my daughter, ex-wife,
And step daughters.
Even those things that I loose, you still hold dear to your hand.
Many times people can't understand,
How could pain be a part of your plan?

Even Judahs Iscariot is methodical,
An integral piece to your overall plan.
I give all of my trust to you
Why even try to understand.
Just use me Lord for today
And again I'll anticipate your return tomorrow!
Patiently waiting for the day
When you return
To take us home to the Father.

Prostituting The Gift 08-12-2011

How many of us has God given something special?
That we sell for material gain,
Or only use to find favor with earthly man!
God gave me this ability to rap
Yet I sell it for so much less than His plan.
My ability to inspire inspiration in the youth!
Just one more talent ran down into the sand.
Singing and dancing, but for myself and not the Lord's work.
Yes! I can hear these animals talk,
But this world tells me that I Am absurd.
Certified to deliver babies,
Yet who is it that will pay the best for this work?
Ordained to deliver conscienceness unto the people,
But right after the collection plate collects!
Football? Or basketball!
Who is it that gives my body this chemistry?
To even have this grace?
Watch the order of my words;
Now the world is out to buy them all.
How much talent I have to produce videos?
And direct movie clips! Watch this tic toc yall.
Building bridges or constructing roads,
Bet I can do it!
From governor to mayor
I can even be the president of America
This wealth puts me above it all.
When it all falls down,
And the money is no longer left
Who is it that I will point to?

And thank you for blessing me with this gift to look to what's next.

Eating With The Enemy 08-14-2011

Have you ever invited satan into God's house?
And told him to sit down to eat with you and the King?
There's been so many times that
satan has come unwelcomed onto me.
I just want to invite him to sit at my fathers house.
To sit down and eat in the presence of the King.
With bills to pay, my children away
And no guarantee of my next way to eat.
Family member just died, The judge lied,
And the world constantly out to get me!
Beyond all of these situations
To keep all focus maintained on the King.
Ignoring the darkness,
And praising the name of the Lord.
Making the old evil one uncomfortable
Until he just wants to get up and run for the door.
To simply flee from this presence
Not as much to say with the King in this space.
Hoped for me to be overcome by burdensome circumstances
But only brought homecourt advantage my way

Please Don't Let Me Die 08-21-2011

When my road becomes rugged, and your path
I can't quite see.
When my family and friends all decide
To turn around and give up on me.
When I've stayed up all night
As a watchman waiting on you!
When I've given you all of my faith
Put all of my hope in you!
When my dreams seem to burden me
And this life brings me down!
Wondering why
From my kids I'm gone away
And their mom won't answer the dial.
Believing in you for the bills
And can't afford to pay the rent.
I know the kingdom lives within,
But it's cold out here in this!
Snow up to my neck
And my head's becoming frostbit!
Your word says is anything too hard?
Yet and still I want to quit.
Your word says satan has no authority;
Like Jesus,
Why is it I that you forsake?
Please dont let me down,
dont let my voice pass away.

The Energy Of Today   08-24-2011

Today how are the stars aligned?
In what formation may the planets be?
The reason for my concern!
Is to know how will this all influence me!
My God is always the same,
But people will always change.
Today will me and my brother get along?
Or will me and my sister not speak again?
What is the magnetic field that creates these polarities?
And how can this fate I change!
Prayer and thinking good thoughts for thee,
Speaking Godly wisdom through your name!
Using the radiance from the Son
To bring life into me!
Just when I had almost given up
The sunshine decided to break through and rescue me.
What causes my soul to grow?
The times while I Am sleep? Or during the strain?
All of this tugging back and forth,
On my small, human brain.
Does my longitude? Or my latitude
Have anything to do with my attitude today!
At times I will to simply take a spacship out to space!
Just meditate until I find myself.
The self that is deep within this quiet space.
A place where I can scrape all of these deep roots away
The want is just to begin again,
Cutting all of the unnecessary away.
Energy will beam!
What is it that will flow your way?
When you walk past me,
How electrical are the impulses
What type of currents flow mine and your way?

When I Become Free 08-23-2011

See me with these chains on my heart
Shackles governing my mind.
The more I search for this key
The more I realize it's so hard to find.
Afraid to let it all go
Just let the old me pass away.
I have to go to work,
I have all of these bills to pay!
I have to do this,
And I have no time for that!
Once this freedom is gone,
There will be no buying it back!
Who is there that can unlock this world?
To open up the new me?
Scared to become my best self;
Too anxious to allow the old self to become the new me.
Let death come onto the old he!
When the King walks through
However is it possible, that I could not be free to do?
Until material wealth,
Family and friends mean nothing to me!
Just a piece in His universe
Hoping to play off of the better part of me.
We are all made of the same thing;
The inward parts!
What components of that tree still reside deep within the me!
Waiting for the flower to blossom
With the help of a bee!
The sun and the moon!
Are all essential parts of the sea.
Compare you to a star,
And how similar will the chemical makeup be!

You are the universe!
Don't be afraid to shine.
Just a temple for G-o-d
Those who have eyes will see,
And those who have ears shall hear
True freedom lives within
Because the King lives here!

Gird up your loins, and fight toward the truth.
Illusions attempt to scare us by fear,
So the King's light can't shine through.
My inward thoughts will eventually become
The overall aura in here.
What do you practice when by yourself?
Thoughts of negative or positivity?
Faith of fear?
Why do we train our brain
When there's not even much light in this day left?
My spirit and soul says we must prepare
For what is to come next.
Today is just the combination
Of my thoughts from yesterday!
This week, this month, this year!
Looking back
What is it that your thought have made!
A long list of changed lives
Or a list of people who don't want to come your way
If the energy we carry is so contagious
Why are we not more careful of what we make!
The strength we use to conqure today
Will surely spill over into tomorrow's ways.
I'm not sure about tomoorow,
Yet I know God's grace is sufficient for today.

Above Emotion 08-30-2011

My universe moves in unison
Each portion in alignment with Gods will.
How many times have you seen a rain storm angry,
Or the suns health ill?
Does the wind get sad?
Or water hold a gloomy face?
We call fire fierce,
When it is only feeding its face!
We all have jobs to do
Ordered by the divine nature of God.
It's the emotional we must rise above,
Or the spiritual will get robbed.
Emotions leave us spiritually paralyzed,
Unable to do God's work.
The evil one knows our weaknesses
Then he puts his goons to work.
Stripping us of our divine nature
Holding us farther away from God!
My God never loses his temper,
And you have the same spirit nature of God!
Yes my flesh is unable
And there is nothing that spirit can't do,
But this power takes on a whole new meaning
When this spirit is in line with you!
Know me to be an ambassador!
Simply a spokesperson for you!
No matter what it is the situation I find me in
My heart stays focused upon you!

Who Can't See 08-30-2011

Persecuted for the work I must do
By the same ones who stand to benefit the most.
Stephen, Jesus, or Martin Luther King;
Standing up for inequalities,
When those who protect and serve are out to capture you.
My sorrow comes not from the crime I've done
But the sin that separated the God from me.
Now how do I get back?
Into the presence of the King!
Please allow me the blood;
The only thing to rinse this filth from me!
Bourn into the world
Where my tradition taught sin to live within me,
Thank you God!
That you allowed Jesus to step in!
Became the new light
Bread to this hungry world we living in!
Most are still blind and deaf,
But how many shall overcome?
Still slayed by the masses,
The ones who can't understand what's been done.
Our father is spiritual wisdom,
Tradition simply piggy backs on old beliefs.
Ideas and ideologies of those not made
In image nor likeness of He.
To put on the mind of the creator,
But who taught Jesus to read?
My God allowed the mind of Christ
To become the whole of me.
At times I sit the book aside,
Meditating until the spirit devours me!
Finding myself close to God
Is what empowers me.

Although right now I don't have much!
Sacred is this small seed to me.
So many can only see what's in my hand now,
But I can see the tree that one day will be.

Don't try to figure out what other people want to hear from you;
figure out what you have to say.

Barbara Kingsolver

When the winds keep beating,
    We will remain,
        Anchored in the lord.
When the waves keep crashing,
    We will remain,
        Anchored in the lord.
When the skies are grey and the son feels so far away,
    We will remain,
        Anchored in the lord.
When it seems as if it will never quit reigning,
    We will remain,
        Anchored in the lord.
When the weather is bitter cold and all others decide to fold
    We will remain,
        Anchored in the lord.
When the sea just seems too deep,
And the en-a-me is right inside of me
    We will remain,
        Anchored in the lord.
When the promise just looks too tough to be fulfilled,
    We will remain,
        Anchored in the lord.
When the en-a-me promises that he knows a better way
    We will remain,
        Anchored in the lord.
When there looks to be no gas left,
And there's still 500 miles left to go
    We will remain,
        Anchored in the lord.

When fear and doubt comes, and there's only wilderness to our
Right and to the left.
>We will remain,
>>Anchored in the lord.
When family and friends leave, and all that is left is me and the
Jesus That I cannot physically see.
>We will remain,
>>Anchored in the lord.
When He calls me to where He is and there are 100 places that I'd
Rather be!
>We will remain,
>>Anchored in the lord.
When the enemy surrounds and the hills look bare
>We will remain,
>>Anchored in the lord.
When the captors tell us to sing, and we know that we're in this
Strange place.
>We will remain,
>>Anchored in the lord
When I'm talking to God, and only wanting to see his face
>We will remain,
>>Anchored in the lord
When we're tired of this hell and ready to leave this wicked place
>We will remain,
>>Anchored in the lord.
When He still has so much work for us to do, but we're so confused
>We will remain,
>>Anchored in the lord.

God's Way 09-24-2011

What is the last big plan you dreamed up?
Of the miracles and wonders that you'd do for God!
How many times did that plan go well?
And on how many occasions do we end up robbed?
Even our best attempt, could never be enough,
Not stacking up to the thought's of God.
Do you know how much more powerful we will be?
If we can learn how to surrender into the will of God?
Six months led by Jesus
Will bear more fruit than I can in 10 lifetimes on my own!
When the branch is attached to His true living vine
How many grapes shall grow?
To become closer and closer to the will of God,
Draw nearer to the voice of the divine.
How strong is your relationship with The Lord!
To become as close as Jesus is a goal of mine,
Living this life by my Father's word!
No thought of what I may be able to do for me,
Just want to live life succombed in His word.
How much time do you spend alone per day to think?
Simply bettering your relation with the Lord?
Now how much time do you spend per day
Becoming better acquainted with the ways of the world?
Vs listening to the will of God's way.

They say that the old me has passed away
That I Am a creature made all new.
Now that I am no longer thinking with my carnal mind
What is it that I'm supposed to do?
No more pleasure comes from what I see,
My filthy hands have been washed all clean!
To be transformed by the renewing of the mind
Now all I can think about is, the you living within me.
What was it like on the cross?
Or praying in the garden?
Thank you Jesus, for allowing me
The ability to move back into the presence of the Father.
So many shadows of the old testament
To show forth in the new.
If your life is of the shadow that
We're now living in
I must spend more of my personal time in prayer with you.
How much is too much studying?
When have I become too intimate with your word!
The things that my friends now want me to do...
Sound absolutely absurd.
Where did this new mind come from?
And how did it choose to enrapture me?
To submit my will onto the Lord,
Resist the devil, and he must flee!
This new way of thinking, is something special,
Much higher than me.
Thank you God for your forgiveness,
For this change you've allowed to transpire
Deep down in the spirit of me.

She Speaks to Me Everywhere 10-07-2011

Can you see the trail that She leaves behind?
By the blowing in the trees
Just watch the clouds roll on bye,
Or the crashing of the waves on the beach.
Listen to the birds sing,
Or watch as the ants do their work.
Have you ever seen an eagle flying overhead?
Effortlessly She soars,
With very little work.
From the miracle of childbirth,
To the breakdown of my DNA.
She speaks to me everywhere!
I hear Him stronger and stronger with each passing day.
Have you seen the love in my heart?
Or the joy in a smile.
Ever seen anyone,
Joyously willing to walk that extra mile?
She speaks to me everywhere!
No matter where I may currently be:
Heaven, hell, or the Jackson state penitentiary.
She speaks to me everywhere.
Whether asleep or in my dreams!
Where ever this spirit dwells
She has already promised to be!

"For since the creation of the world Her invisible attributes are
clearly seen, being understood by the things that are made, even
Her eternal power and Godhead, so that they are without excuse,"
Romans 1:20

Let It Dance   10-10-2011

"Do you not know that your bodies are members of Christ?....Or do you not know that your body is the temple of the Holy Spirit who is in you, whom you have from God, and you are not your own? For you were bought at a price; Therefore glorify God in your body and in your spirit, which are God's."

1 Corinthians 6:15, 19-20

How could we not praise His name
For what has been placed in our DNA!
It's the blood of Jesus
That even allows us to see just one more day
Nothing that could have been done by the self,
But what is already pre-ordained.
Just decided to let it all go;
Let the Holy Spirit guide my way.
Dancing and praising!
Like there is no tomorrow.
No idea what it is that has come over,
But why even bother?
My finite mind would never even understand
Just let the spirit praise G-o-d;
And dance.

My Heart Sings 10-11-2011

Find me captured in the land of my oppressors
Working at slave wages!
Wondering will this toil ever end?
Just like my Jesus, but never to the same degree;
My captors constantly torment and curse at me.
Aint I a brother! At other times, am I even a human being?
My biblical reading speaks reality
So why are they constantly trying to brand this six digit number
in to me? No, I wont accept it, remember it,
Or engrave it into my brain.
My God leaves His mark on the forehead
So I remain focused on eternity instead.
Still my heart sings unto the lord
For letting me cultivate your land!
Still my heart sings unto the lord
For allowing me to be just a small part of your larger plan.
Never will these captors steal my joy;
The world didn't give it, And the world can't take it away.
Praise be to you lord!
For letting the Son shine bright
For at least Won more day.
With all of your creation,
Reaching up toward your greatness
Why not would I?
My mind stays focused on meeting with you,
High up in the sky.
At times, I travel into space
To remove the self from this place.
And to glory in your greatness
The vast wealth of such empty, quiet space!
'Let there be light' and now we have the days.
My captors think I Am trapped here,
But my heart sings out to you God
214   With each and every passing day.

For The Hope Of Israel
I Am Bound With This Chain
Acts 28:20 10-12-2011

Murderers, thieves, dope sellers and baby rapers!
This Israel is all tainted, and here I Am in the midst of it!
Guilty as charged, so my plea never allowed a trial.
Tribulation brought these persecutions not only to me,
But the ripple effect shows on all it involved!
Now that I live in this boneyard
What Am I to do!
Decide to bow down and give my birthright onto you!
With my mind focused on the lord,
I set my destination on home.
Although I came here alone
Look how many are turning
And following me back home to my Lord.
Though The world won't forgive,
Jesus only said sin no more.
I Am the only way
You can come into me through only that door.
Thanks to you! I am a disciple,
Bringing others unto the light!
Have you seen many candles in conjunction?
The light becomes more and more bright.
Until all darkness has been revealed and exposed.
Some will still find crevices,
Not quite ready yet to go.
But those that have been called by my Fathers will
Are the ones that I hold dear to my soul.
Ready to create new beginnings
With testamonies from night to light.
If My God will save these...
Then what can be too hard for Her might?

The Will To Survive 10-13-2011

When the pain begins to run deep.
Gnawing deep into the soul.
What exactly is it that pushes us, the way that we will go?
To hold on by faith, or give up in despair?
Live God's life with no worries!
Or lose my cool over a misplaced hair?
Emotions in us are dangerous,
If not properly used.
Through all that Jesus went through
I can only think of once where he lost his cool.
What wills us to keep on goin?
Though the devil stands in our face.
Mind focused on God.
Dilligently set out on finishing your race.
With Our Father bigger than everything,
How would anything weigh us down?
These obstacles set before me.
Only serve as one more barrier to get around.
How could I not scale this wall,
With the lord as my trust?
Why can't I walk atop of this bobed wire fence?
Without getting all cut up!
The Lord is my protector, so I shall not fear.
The angels came to break this soul out,
But when my physical awoke; I'm still in here.
Grasping to find the balance,
Between the physical and spiritual worlds!
The spirit and soul keep battling,
Fighting the ways of this world.
The only way to eradicate lies, is to know absolute truths.
We don't have to worry about which voice is guiding,
When we're solely focused on you!

Toe To Toe 10-15-2011

Looking at the enemy in the face
Expecting me to back down!
Like I don't know It's the true and living
Word that resounds;
I stay strapped now.
9-millimeter, A.K. or call it a banger.
King James version is the bullets that I'm out here slanging.
Simply a soldier for my lord:
Adorned in this maize and blue robe;
Purple silk to be my headband;
The glory is Hers for all to behold,
Give to others the silver and gold.
I'm known to keep on fighting,
Anything to finish this race.
Not to the biggest or the strongest
But to those who know God is the author of this fate.
My lord gives all authority;
We are the true rulers of this place.
Your deception could never be enough
To turn me away!
The lord has me trained to be a killer;
devils die everyday.
This fight is bigger than you or me,
Like Muhammad Ali in the ring;
I Am a figure head, the spokesperson for many.
Here I Am now. An ambassador for the king.
Trained my whole life for this fight.
Never will I stay down on my knees
Down here lowly is me.
Until I get back home where my heavenly father holds the keys!

What reason may you have,
To give life your all?
Use that to keep on fighting,
Even when it may seem too small.
A mustard seed is all that it takes
So just keep the faith.
Find a way to maintain
For just one more day.
Tomorrow may bring new hope,
A new reason to believe.
One foot placed afront of the other
Is the only way we will achieve.
The journey of 1,000 miles, begins all by faith.
The hope is that we can make it
And moving forward is the only way.
Be it inch by inch,
Or mile by mile
We will make it to the intended destination
Even if it takes some extra time.
The true fight begins within;
Having faith when we can see no other way.
Begin to live life as if there is no tomorrow.
Live life as if there is only today.

At The Point of Death 10-19-2011

What do we do when we've cum so far,
But can only think of how much traveling we still have left?
When the fear begins to set in,
And the self just wants to turn back.
To move to familiar territory; Known surroundings.
Scared of what lies ahead,
At this unchartered grounds we're surrounded in.
Jesus didn't even have to go,
"Your son still lives."
So the noble man went his way and,
His child was blessed to breathe again.
Because in Jesus word he believed
Who are the ones that need signs and wonders?
In order to believe.
So many haven't even seen the holes,
But still we believe.
How much is too much?
When you feel you just have nothing left.
Without water or food, we refuse to take one more step!
How do we be like Jesus?
"I have food to eat of which you do not know."
Only focused on the fathers will,
So we continue to grow.
Gathering a harvest.
Knowing our testamony
Because it's His words that we speaking in.
Slumped over in despair,
Do I dare? Or dare not go?
Too much invested to turn back,
The Father's voice is all I know.
Urging me forward,
Motivating me on.
Just got to keep on moving
Until this feeling of death is gone.   219

When God's Hand Comes in   10-26-201--

"Therefore humble yourselves under the mighty hand of God, that
He may exalt you in due time."

1 Peter 5:6

Feeling that I've done all that I can do
Knowing that I can move no further than where I am
Wondering what is the meaning of your plan?
And how to remove this burden from mortal man.
Why do I feel so heavy, If your burden is so light?
Still can't put this down,
Though I try with all of my might.
Ready to face death
Find me at the point of can't quit.
Ready to subdue onto your will.
To get this all over with
After so much time of trying to do it my way.
How many times will I try?
Before I admit that this isnt working.
Your ways are higher than my ways,
Hand it all over to the crown.
No more mind set on me
Only thoughts of you have abound.
Watching as all of my troubles move away
Because of you: It is done.
More trust and more belief, by the more that I see.
Lord I believe! help my unbelief.
After toiling all night,
My troubles only seemed to outgrow me.
Immediately they disappeared when my focus shifted beyond me.
Thank you Jesus for coming, to save me from this world
Giving me the way back
For us, opening up that door.
Now nothing is impossible,
Because we can find our way back through you.

Blessed Through Troubled Waters 10-24-2011

Who says life is to be easy?
It's the troublesome times that have generated the most
Character in me.
Stagnant life is equal to standing around Bethesda
Waiting to see what the angels stirring of the water will bring.
How could we enjoy the serenity of calm waters?
When we've never seen the storm?
Some of us will only see from a distance,
While others will be caught in the midst of the storm.
How many of your troubled situations
Proved to be a miracle at a meeting later?
We should never be surprised by what happens
When we maintain a positive attitude
And only move forward by faith in our maker.
What is it that you will need?
When Jesus sees you lying there
Prostate on your face.
In your condition for such a long time
And he asks, "Do you want to be made well?"
Will we gripe and complain
Of having no one to place us in the stirred well?
Or simply believe in all faith.
When the un-seen Jesus extends to us his almighty right hand?
"Rise, take up your bed and walk."
And immediately be made well.
Through my troublesome situation
I can only see a blessing.
Simply waiting for the testimony that I will have to tell.

"It is not the healthy who need a doctor, but the sick."

Luke 5:29-31

The Pharisees spent all of their time clicked up
Only wanting to be around their own.
Jesus let go of a mighty kingdom
To be of the many that were not of his own.
How perfect blood, could dwell with sinners and tax collectors?
They could not see.
The King of Jerasulem, sent here to save you and me.
Your filth must not touch us, we are above thee.
How many friends did Jesus have? In this text we read
I bet I will come back.
Thank you God for saving me.

"Greater love has no one than this, than to lay down one's life for his friends. You are my friends If you do whatever I command you."

John 15:13-14

It Aint Over 10-30-2011

You may of won the battle
With all hopes that I would fight no more.
My Lord's is the biggest battle
That was lost in the physical,
But victorious in the spiritual world.
My God always has a plan,
So know that this aint over.
This war is to be much bigger than that!
To still have faith, through all that you may have stolen:
Wife; Kids; and Career!
Thanks to my God He made you spare my life.
Now we create one more testament for goodness
While rebuilding this broken down rite.
Torn down to the weakest point,
But never to the point of giving up.
It is when we are the weakest,
That God is the most strong within us.
You meant for this to hurt me,
But my Father used it to do good!
In earth as it is in heaven;
Even in your world my God rules.
Knowing this war is much bigger than me,
I pray to take my place in this current time.
This war started in heaven,
Then from hell into this paradise I climbed.
Well it aint over!
Till this war is completely won.
Never giving up,
Patiently waiting until comes the Son.

Our doubts are traitors, and make us lose the good we oft might win, by fearing to attempt

William Shakespeare

Simply Believe   10-26-2011

In the darkest of life's trials,
During the climax of our deepest temptations.
What exactly is it?
That will decide if we will fall off,
Or continue to make it?
When evil thoughts are in my mind
And no one else seems to care.
How to get to the roots of this tree
And have them all removed from there!
Planting new seed,
Don't show many results among the weeds and tares.
Many will grow, some will die!
But the crop will turn out so much better
if at first, the land is made bare.
Lord show me how to cultivate,
Submit me to your will.
Got me yoked as a young to an old Ox
Until I learn to flow with your will.
The whole time believing!
That through this training I will become You.
Taking off the old man
And becoming all new.

When The Goal Is Just Too Great   10-28-2011

What is it that you won't do?
When giving your all to the goal!
To completely lose track of all surroundings,
And mental fortitude begins to take control.
Here's to no more physical pain,
And emotions gone astray.
The intended intent is to do a hostile takeover;
For all of the unbelief to be choked away.
No way to be denied. Turn back, Or
Talked into turning around.
Simply to move forward by reckless abandon
Letting the spirit move the physical in the correct way.
Not even quite sure if this is what the I
Needs to do.
But the higher power has taken over my way:
Foaming at the mouth;
And in a paralyzed state;
This brain has shut down;
Control is from a remote!
In outter space.
Must reach the intended destination!
To only reach the goal.
Something in me has the dial set
There is no way it would ever take no.
When the goal set in the mind is just too great,
We know where every inch of energy must go.
At the goal line with fourth and inches.
Tripple overtime in the winters cold.
Losing is not an option.
Over the competition we must go.
When the goal is too great
You will find the way home.

The Wise Farmer 10-29-2011

Who would plant seeds in a plot untilled!
First the ground must be cultivated
Some even implant it with nitrogen.
Got the ground on steroids. Before implanting my seed.
Waiting until the time is just right
Universe supplying all that I need.
Some will give up early, before the plant has even begun.
Too impatient to let the seed take root.
So focused on the harvest yet to cum.
Some won't continue to water,
Giving the seed what it needs to grow.
Continue to till the earth
Air is needed in that earth to grow.
Down on my knees, plucking each weed by hand.
In all attempts to keep these out of here,
So the enemy can't impede on the plan.
Scarecrow may be necessary,
To deter the outside feeders from entering.
Keeping this garden fenced in,
To ward off unwanted visitors!
One with nature! Is the way we ought to be.
I feed the universe,
And in turn, the Universe feeds me.
The wise or the full farmer?
Which one do you dare to be?
My only hope is to get better
Throughout my spiritual maturity!

"Rescue Me" 11-07-2011

With so many around me drowning
Do I only save myself?
I can hear His voice telling me to dive in
But disaster looks to be coming next!

"Go and say to my people, you will hear my words, but you will not
understand; You will see what I do, but you will not perceive it's
meaning. For the hearts of these people are hardened, and their
ears cannot hear, And they have closed their eyes. So their eyes
cannot see, And their ears cannot hear, And their hearts cannot
understand, and they cannot turn to me and let me heal them."

ACTS 28:26-27

Well if these drowning dare not to be saved,
What's the point of going back anyway?

"She is a voice shouting in the wilderness: Prepare a pathway for
the Lords coming! Make a straight road for him! Fill in the val-
ley's, and level the mountains and hills! Straighten the curves, and
smooth out the rough places! And then all people will see the salva-
tion sent from God."

Luke 3:4-6

Yes Lord,
And I dived right in.

Stop Running 11-06-2011

"Then the lord God called to Adam and said to him, "Where are you?" So he said, "I heard your voice in the garden, and I was afraid because I was naked; And I hid myself."

Genesis 3:9-10

How many times must She save us?
Yet we still running away.
Repeating over and over again,
While She's calling out your fate.
Knows you by name. Yet you still think it's luck.
Not just done on a whim,
We turn and go back to Him.
Then turn around and do the same thing all over again.
How many times must it take,
Before we will truly learn?
How many times must She save,
Before deciding to let the whole damn city burn?
If you find me just 10!
I shall spare the whole city.
The angels are here to warn us,
Yet we continue to ignore the heavenly messages that they bringing.
Stop running from the lord,
Knowing that you hear Her voice!
Simply repent for the sin,
Yes we do have the choice.
Hiding in the foilage,
Attempting to cover up our sin.
Where is there that I can hide from God?
He is our best friend.
Why seek the advice of others? When they only know trouble.
Get down to your knees and tell the father that you love him!

I'm sorry for blowing mine inheritance;
Spending on prodigal living.
Now allow me to only be your servant!
After spending so much time in this prison.
I only want to provide for you a service
Ministered in your name
Living this life as if i've already been pre-ordained.
Simply stop Running,
And take your whole life to God.
Just put all else down,
When She's calling you out to life.

"'For this my son was dead and is alive again; He was lost and is
found,' And they began to be merry."

Luke 15:24

The Black Rose 11-08-2011

Just because I've never seen you
Does not mean that you do not exist:
Pink; Red; White; and Yellow everywhere.
But how bizzar is this??
The rose that grew from concrete
Is truly the color of me.
Now not only through the use of imagination,
My brother's work adds new life unto me.
Beautiful you are
And rare in American form!
I found your fairness in Switzerland!
My America has never showed me love.
Beauty is in the color of me!
Even if from so far away.
But why you don't let me bloom in the
White house garden?
Is a topic for another day.
Thank you America!
For trying to hide these beautiful foliage away;
The truth will be revealed.
No matter how hard you try to wash it away.

Who Killed Mike 11-08-2011

America is the culprit!
Though Conrad takes the blame.
Although the true bully
Hides in the background again
My America needs a face! Well then point the finger,
And say that's the bad guy.
Well it was Mike who was the won
You were teasing; Just before he was taken under.
What need would there have been for propofol
If we never raped him of his world!
Accused of child molestation!
After all he did so much for young boys and girls!
The scared crowd, always laughs at the vicious bully
Until he takes it too far!
How much fun did America have
Watching another one of our greats fall?
How dumb are we? To also throw Conrad away.
With one stone throw,
America takes Away two more of our greats!
How many must fall, before we truly will see what's going on?
Who killed Mike?
The same thief that sent
Tupac and Big home!
Whose face is in the background?
Covered and hidden away.
How could we ever trust in this system?
For true justice anyway
When this system wasn't built to bring true justice onto us.
For true justice!
When for no reason,
So many of us have been taken back to dust?

"I Don't Remember Them Anymore" 11-13-2011

"No more shall every man teach his neighbor, and every man his brother, saying, 'Know the Lord,' For they all shall know me, from the least of them to the greatest of them, says the lord. For I will forgive their iniquity, and their sin I will remember no more."

Jeremiah 31:34

What sin may you be holding dear to heart?
That the enemy will not let pass away?
Tonight only ask the spirit to bring them to rememberance
So we can repent...And tomorrow is to be a new day:
Keep back your servant also, from presumptuous sins;
Let them not have dominion over me.
As far as the east is from the west
Has man seen the depth of the ocean beneath?
You have set our iniquities before you,Our secret sins in the light of Your countenance
But our iniquities have separated us from our God;
And our sins have hidden his face from us
So it is that he will not hear.
For this is my covenant with them, when I take away their sins
For I delivered to you first of all that which I also received:
That Christ died for our sins according to the scriptures.
And if Christ is not risen, your faith is futile;
You are still in your sins!
In him we have redemption through his blood,
The forgiveness of sins, according to the riches of his grace
So Christ was offered once to bear the sins of many.
To those who eagerly wait for him He will appear a second time,
Apart from sin, for salvation.
If we confess our sins to Jesus Christ,
She is faithful, and just to forgive us our sins.
And to cleanse us from all unrighteousness.
And She herself is the propitiation for our sins,
And not only for ours only, but also for the whole world.

234

I write to you, Little children,
Because your sins are forgiven you for His name's sake.

"He will again have compassion on us, and will subdue our
Iniquities. You will cast all our sins into the depth of the sea."

Micah 7:19

References:
Psalm 90:8
Isaiah 59:2
Romans 11:27
1 Corinthians 15: 3 & 17
Ephesians 1:7
Hebrews 9:28
1 John 9

The Well That Refreshens 11-14-2011

When the journey seems to be too much
And the thought through the mind is, 'No more'.
What is there that will keep us going,
Or even by faith,
Put us down on our knees
As we patiently wait through the storm?
With the mind focused on home,
What other place is there to go?
With the mind set on a destination
The body is sure to go.
What is the well that keeps us anew?
Cleansing the soul in the midst of the muck.
Washing us free of our yesterdays;
Remembering our iniquities no more!
Yesterday is simply a mystery,
The living well does not work in the past,
His spirit is only of the present and
The future is not guaranteed to come to pass.
How can one keep such faith?
After much fighting
Not even being halfway there.
The hope is that the Lord will show in an instant
And immediately, we will be there.

When Everything Reminds Me of You 11-16-2011

I was reading a book today,
Urging my young student to pull through.
Of all of the names in the world?
However could this last name
Be in the likeness of you!
Flooding my mind and invading my inward thoughts
How could I ever pull you away?
Not that I do, but if I wanted to
How do I ever move you away?
My soul knows no more meaning to the word ME
There is only you and us.
From watching TV,
To reading the bible!
Everything I do
Brings to mind joyous thoughts of us!
Even our "Bad" situations,
Only bring about our amassed good.
Knowing that we will pull through this by faith.
Thank you God for the strength to only make it through.
With yesterday's all gone,
To the future it is
That I point my faith.
Your love for me is everything,
The reason to not give up in this wicked place.
Thank you for loving me
Know that you're always on my mind.
Lord please don't move that mountain,
Only give us the strength to climb

Run The Rise 11-16-2011

How much faith do you have?
What's your reason to continue movin on?
When the mind can only see the light at the end of the tunnel,
But in front of me there are only big buildings,
And detour signs.
With only faith left to continue to run,
When there seems to be not much time left
My God will cause us to rise!
With only a dead end left, and the enemy
Trailing close behind.
A 20 foot stone wall ahead of me,
And no ladder in order to climb.
What is there to lift us above?
When physically there is no way to left or right.
To close the eyes and only see greatness
Knowing that the spiritual is the only way that we have life.
What's the moral to the story?
Run then rise!
Could this be only a test of my faith?
Gods way of making my inner warrior mentality cum to rise!
Who was able to rise above?
Without first having the faith to continue to climb.
The physical meaning of things here
Are not quite the same on the spiritual side:
Refined by fire;
Lions eating straw;
Chariots moving up into heaven;
All of the spiritual things that John saw!
How strong is your belief?
To see this world through Jesus' eyes?
Put your dreams upon his back, and
Go out and run then rise.

He Aint Finished 11-16-2011

From dining with the heads of state
To counting heads of sheep.
Moses thought it was all over,
So to the wilderness he decided to flee.
From Ivy league to the cotton patch;
Have you ever thought that you were being held back?
From the oval office to a taxi cab
How many of us can relate to that?
From swinging a gold golf club to digging a ditch;
However did I get myself into this?
From state police to facing multiple felonies;
How could I ever come into this?
What is your humbling situation?
The glitch thrown into your final plan?
No matter how many times we may have felt it permanant
God's voice says, "This is not my final plan."
Simply preparing you for what I need you to do
Moses preparation took 40 years,
While 40 days is what Jesus needed to go through.
Who knows what I may need for my training here?
The real reason I was placed into the devils place.
Complaining won't move me anywhere
So I simply remain.
Grateful for this path,
While continuing to keep all faith!
Study all that I can, while housed in this wicked space.
No matter how hopeless it may look,
Knowing that God aint finished with you yet.
Attitude determines altitude
Don't give up on Him yet.
Just keep the faith in yourself.
She aint finished with you yet.

Have you ever been nudged by an angel?
Advising you to head south?
Did you listen to the words,
Or ignore the heavenly words coming out of it's mouth?
Chasing down a chariot!
Did you decide not to go?
Or to believe?
Listening to words given from the spirit!
Or convincing the self, 'She can't be talking to me.'
If the Lord tells you to go
Then the meeting is already pre-ordained to be.
Be it chasing down a chariot, a vehicle,
A spaceship or an airplane.
With men this is impossible,
But by God we will do all things.
When evil attempts to talk you out of it
Get up and run by the Lords instructed means.
Once you do get there
The question is always the same,
"Do you underdstand what you are reading?"
"How can I unless someone teaches me."
Replies the ethiopian man.

Optimism is a perfectly legitimate response to failure

Stephen King

Don't Move That Mountain 11-17-2011

"The mountains melt like wax at the presence of the lord, at the presence of the lord of the whole earth. The heavens declare His righteousness, and all the peoples see His glory."

Psalm 97:5-6

Please Lord don't move that mountain
Although from here it looks so high!
Please Lord Don't move that mountain
I only ask that you give me the strength to climb.
Be it going over or crawling under,
I only ask that you lead me the correct way.
Please Lord don't move that mountain,
I only ask that you give me the strength as in Paul's faith!
Lord don't move that mountain;
Joseph's fate was turned around.
Please grant me the strength lord,
To get up after each and every time that I may fall down.
Please Lord don't move that mountain.
By faith I know you can remove that huge mound.
Allow me to hold faith higher than fear,
And that big mountain is only a small pile.
Lord don't move that mountain
I know that you would never give up on me now.
Where there is a will, there is a way
Please grant Peter's belief unto me now!
I can, I will.
I must not give up on me now:
To just make it half way,
And I trust that you will throw me some heavenly rope down.
Lord don't move that mountain,
Although from here it looks so high.
Lord don't move that mountain,
I only ask that you give me the strength to climb.

"So He answered and said to me: "This is the word of the lord to Zerubbabel: 'Not by might nor by power, but by my spirit,' says the lord of hosts. 'Who are you, O great mountain? Before Zerubbabel you shall become a plain! And She shall bring forth the capstone- with shouts of "Grace, grace to it!""""

Driving us Mad 11-23-2011

Got us locked in this place, with nothing else to do
Took out vocational trades, and took out college courses too!
Now what else are criminals supposed to do?
Call this reformation!
But you aint helping me.
Got our anger up on high in here
Hoping that freedom will never ring!
Thank you Jim Crow, for setting this trap of mental slavery.
It's been how many years later?
And yet you still enslaving me!
The one thing you didn't expect
Was to see so many of your own kind:
Stuck in this here rut, right here with me;
Trapped in this maze called corrections;
Doing hard time.
Still trapped in this place, no matter how high we can climb
Got so many bound by this revolving door,
Stuck spinning around, stuck in crime!
How best to relieve pent up frustration?
My wife's love is not allowed while doing time!
When correction officers can't stand prisoners,
And the warden hates men.
How do you expect me to turn my life around?
Jesus is my best friend.
Thank you God for your peace.
Jesus for keeping me sane.
The Holy Spirit for allowing me the strength to get through
For just one more day.
Rehibilitation is what you expect of me
When all I see is prisoners bored.
With so much idle time and idle minds
Which options are we expected to explore!

Take away everything!
Even good time no more.
Locked away in Michigan penitentiary
Praying that one day they will open these doors.

Prison Dreams 11-25-2011

Bentley, Ferrari, and even a Jag!
Mansions in Michigan, California, Florida,
And a Jersey flat.
New York high rise!
Flying in and out of the states;
G-6 status for when we headed out of state.
Search ye the kingdom and all else shall be added unto you!
Million dollar tithes to the church!
Yeah, we do that monthly too.
College funds and charity work!
Endowment funds to give.
Money allotted to other nations,
Used to bring Jesus to the kids.
God is my Father!
None of this is by the likes of me.
Just allow me to be a true shephard and re-distribute
What you've done by me!
No more to financial worries
God has taken them away.
Now we have lots of money to go around.
Plentiful and abundant be our phrase.
Thank you for funneling this way through me.
He who is faithful with little!....
Well thank you for alot.
Billions of dollars we have to spend
Thank you Lord for what we got.

Desparation 11-25-2011

What do you do when you reach your end point?
When you no longer even care?
Knowing this to be a dangerous situation,
And that you must quickly get out of there.
With the mind advising you to move
Yet the physical just wont go.
Attempting to muster up the energy,
But the body just don't want to go.
How to move from this state of depression,
Avoid these times of despair?
Jesus wept.
Although he knew God was right there.
What am I supposed to do?
Though I know that you'll never leave me alone.
Come find me on the mountain top
Looking to the way to enter your throne.
Feel me with your love;
Take this pain away!
My soul is in need of some peace.
And I believe in the narrow way;
Lord help my unbelief!
So wide is this other gate
I know it seems to be wrong,
But so many are already headed this way
Redeem me from such misery.
Clear this confusion in my soul.
Why do you allow this sin to pull me away?
When the spiritual keeps asking me I Am done!
Which way to go?
And in which direction will I find my peace?
I only know that I don't want to be here no more!
Patiently waiting for you to come back to claim me.

Keep Me Pushing 11-26-2011

Feeling like I Am all done.
As if I can go no more.
Deep into enemy territory.
With so much left still to get done.
With no way out,
Wondering what is there left for me to do!
What reasons do I have,
To move forward and complete this duel:
I envision your face,
See your smile in my mind.
In everything that I do
Even from here, I can feel your kisses in my mind;
On home I set my grind.
The thoughts of your love!
Our bodies tangled in every day;
Walks in the park!
Catching butterflies for just one more day;
Home cooked meals;
Now again I'm on the move.
Aprons and high heels!
Gotta make my way home to you;
Snow forts and snow ball fights!
Gotta pass this test;
Story time and bath time,
You bring out all of my best.
Dollar store and Mickey mouse pancakes!
Blueberries and strawberries fresh out of the garden.
So many reasons to move on up out of here;
Focus renewed!
By my visions of you.
I can crawl just a few steps farther.
Dig into your mind,
To find out what moves you.

And You Don't Even See It 11-29-2011

Stuck in this trap
On a one way;
Headed in the opposite direction.
You ask me what I'm mad for,
"It's only because I care for ya.
In you I can see God's reflection."
I see more worth in you than you may even see in yourself
Knowing we can get out of this place,
And I Am right beside ya for help,
But I can't fight it for ya.
What kind of tail are you carrying?
Your time to see the parole board is coming up.
They long to keep you buried here!
For the rest of your young life.
You are my little brother.
I can see the innocence in your eyes.
No we don't have to be criminals
Although we did commit a crime.
We don't have to be inmates
For the rest of our lives.
Yes, you can call me a prisoner,
But I'll only be that to Christ.
Thank you for setting us free.
Not holding us bondage to sin in this life.
You have released our shackles,
Given us forever light from within;
Now thank God we can be yoked with him.
Allow me Jesus to show these brothers
That you are the only way to make it home to Him.

When Night Falls 11-28-2011

"Neither this man nor his parents sinned, "Said Jesus," But this happened so that the work of God might be displayed in his life. As long as it is day, we must do the work of Him who sent me. Night is coming, when no one can work. While I Am in the world, I Am the light of the world."

John 9:3-5

Now that it's dark outside what are we to do?
The work of God still needs to be displayed,
But how to do that without you?
If night has now come when no one is able to work,
Then what exactly is it that keeps us from going bazerk?
By sonlight or moonlight
Your reflection lives within.
Starlight or firelight,
Your words these lips keep singing like hymns.
Hungry for your living well
Though still not sure of what it is;
Have I received it?
Is it in me?
Well, what benefits come with it?
What importance does the sabbath bring?
Can we heal on it too!
The pharisees have multiplied,
And our numbers are still so few.
Is it a sin for working on the sabbath?
How could an ordinary sinner do such miraculous things
As you?
How many will not speak up?
Afraid of what the authority will bring to you!
When night falls too early to snooze.
How are we to shed some light on this darkened thing?
When night falls to early.
How will our Fathers light we bring?
When it is darkness that implores me

"I will deliver you from the jewish people, as well as from the gentiles, to whom I now send you, to open their eyes, In order to turn them from darkness to light, and from the power of satan to God, that they may receive forgiveness of sins and an inheritance among those who are sanctified by faith in me."

Acts 26:17-18

Prove It 12-05-2011

You say with men this is impossible,
But with God we can do all things.
This is Israel.
I Am Gideon.
Here to put out my fleece.
Hoping that through me, you will prove miraculous things.
Do not be angry with me Lord
Let me make just one more request please.
One more test with this fleece!
To be certain that I Am hearing your voice through this thing.
Allow the spirit to come upon me,
So I can be clothed within the power of you through this thing.
To all who believe in Jesus,
This is what is promised to bring.
At times my human nature will experience fear and uncertainty
In difficult circumstances I Am advised to place,
All of my faith,
In you.
From 32,000 to 300, in the Lord all by faith.
Only by a simple fleece Lord, Gideon was encouraged in the way.
They say Abel showed the first act of faith
Enoch walked with God I Am told.
Noah believed God, and obeyed with no questioning.
Abraham trusted in God's love.
I read that Sarah believed in God's promise
Isaac blessed his sons according to the love of the Lord.
Jacobs name was changed to Israel,
And the twelve tribes were of his sons.
If Joseph would have never believed that God
Would someday deliver his people
Would he never have been sold as a slave?
Jochebed and her husband Moses
How are we to know they were so bold and brave?

You tell me Rahab helped the spies,
And that Gideon, Barak, Samson, and Jephthah
Gained strength from God?
The fable says that David killed Goliath.
Samuel led the people of Israel
According to the will of the lord.
How much led up to Jesus?
And now where does that leave us?
Believing in the miracles of God,
And that God's spirit lives deep down within us.
How many have risen from the dead?
And how possible is it that we could see some more?
By faith I believe in you Jesus,
But exactly why! I dont know.
Been told so many things
That never came to pass:
Lied to by my earthly father;
Lied to by my forefathers;
Even at my Uncle Sam I can only laugh.
Yeah Jesus is the reason,
But in America,
Money attempts to govern the seasons.
Through your Son prove it lord.
Even many of your own people are starting to not believe.
Glorify thy self Lord.
There is no other power like you!
Jesus was born to perform miracles
Now what are we to do?
"Peace be still."
And now I patiently wait
Knowing that you will come through with mighty power,
but for now,
We patiently wait.

Pardon me,
Feel free to call me selfish,
But this ones mine.
I Am the king in this love affair,
And She is my queen divine.
Enchanted is this love we share.
Her heart is all and only mine
I Am Her beloved
Like King Solomon,
We will flourish through all the tests of time.
For now you can find me locked away,
Doing hard time:
I can see your tears dying scarlett,
Passing away the time;
Using the wealth to flourish our kingdom!
Growing in heart and mind.
Producing clothing for the kids,
Those who are lost you help to find.
A priestess in your own nature.
A prophetess in this current time.
With God you have divine connection:
Each night your spirit I long to find.

Put It Down   12-12-2011

I've been carrying this for a while
This heavy burdeon about my neck.
Found some pride in this compartment
Envy and lust in the next.
Been carrying these for so long
That it almost feels natural for me here.
Guilt and depression all weighing down so heavily upon me.
I like to hide this one here,
Small enough to hold behind.
'Praise God and halleleujah.'
That was close!
This one they almost did see.
This one has a nice exterior;
Inside it holds all of my dreams.
The more that I get,
The more that I seem to need.
Now how Am I to praise you Lord?
Carrying all of these things.
Each time I attempt to yell out your name,
This strap tightens upon my frame!
Now how do I cum to you Lord?
With so much history bound to these heavy chains.
Tell me what is true worship;
How do I release all of this weight?
No care to look back,
No want to find out where the baggage lands.
Only want to fall down at your feet Lord,
Feel this life fall into your open hands.

I will either find a way, or make one

Hannibal

Over 300 Years Later 12-06-2011

See these lashes across my back?
Watch me carry this pain.
The redness in my eyes
Show's that I've been crying again.
Doing my best to keep my cool,
While bottled up under such heavy oppression.
Asking me to forget my past:
The African Slave Trade;
Separate but equal;
The inside of the American prison system!
How would I ever forget my teachings?
Something so important to my kids future.
Thanks to God I forgive!
But know that I aint stupid.
Who would hang a pregnant woman by her ankles upside down?
Disembowel the kid,
Then stomp on it! Until it lives no more!
Yeah many may not remember,
Too busy still enjoying the benefits.
Who robbed my great great grandfather of his house and land.
And by what authority allowed his killing?
In my dreams I still see pictures
Of faces that I'll possibly never know!
Afraid for the lynchings,
Afraid of what might happen if massa knows!
Don't tell me to bury these skeletons
I don't know what you have buried in your head.
The one thing I can tell you,
Is that the spirit is never dead.
Whose are these voices?
Telling me not to look the other way.
Malcolm was creating a class action law suit!
And like that he was taken away!

What exactly are we hiding?
As the generations pass away.
The warfare is not carnal but spiritual.
Stand still where you are and begin to pray.
Who might you run into?
On your way into hell.
How many in heaven? You never thought you would see there!
Glad you fought for the right thing
Rather than helping to persecute me!
Don't listen to me speak as you read these words.
There's another spirit living within me,
And it needs to scream out and be heard!
How do we ever heal a scar? Or an amputated limb?
When the same knife is allowed back
Over and over again.
Cutting deep on the way in, And tearing as it comes out.
Count these prison numbers
Now the pure white ones divide out!
I guess some are simply bred to be criminals!
Implanted into their DNA.
Some meant to be saved
So far, by this prison, so many are unfairly taken away.
Separate but equal, Mississippi bombings, Rodney and Martin
Luther King.
Harriet Tubman, Marcus Garvey, Malcolm X
Brutally taken up to be with the King.
Yeah, you can tell me that's old,
But can't tell me why Biggey and Tupac were assignated
In the same way.
Black Panthers washed away in a jet stream of violence!
All for trying to help me out today.
If I were to keep your blinders on.

However would I ever begin to truly see? Only accusations!
I know your good at covering up what you've done to me.
Whether here,
Or in the next lifetime,
The stinch of death will Always Come back.
How many are spending life in prison?
For only a dime-rock of crack.
While others were caught with kilos of cocaine!
And only told to never come back.
With no probation, no jailtime, and no papertrail to claim!
Don't even have to check the box!
So over six figures they will still sustain.
So many years later;
This time was proclaimed to be.
The word must become manifest,
God has promised this to you and me:

"But God spoke in this way: That His descendants would dwell in
a foreign land, and that they would bring them into bondage and
oppress them four hundred years. And the nation to whom they
will be in bondage I will judge,
Said God, and after that they shall come out and serve me in this
place."

Acts: 7:6-7

Is It True? 12-12-2011

What's up Bro?

I know that you had a lot of questions,
Before from this world you were allowed to leave.
Just sitting here missing your face
While reading The Rose That Grew From Concrete.
Imagining your energy!
Feeling your electricty through the air
Admiring the influence you still have over people,
More than 20 years later.
So now I want to know:
Does heaven got a ghetto?
And how are you enjoying your thug mansion!
Were the members of the Black Panther Party
There to welcome you?
When you made it up to heaven.
How many were kissing ass to go to heaven
And aint show up?
Is death all that you predicted it would be?
Are you happy to be free from this life?
This is the ballad of a dead soldier!
Have you smoked weed with Christ?
You told us to expect you like Jesus!
Well thank God that neither of you have died!
Through your hands and through music.
You both are right here.

Great Expectancy 12-16-2011

I'm expecting to be released from bondage early!
This is the hope that I have.
I'm expecting to see my father's house at peace,
And financial difficulties to be a thing of the past!
I'm expecting great wealth!
And for my Mother's recouperation to be full and well!
I'm expecting for the people to flock in in masses!
And for the congregation to grow as God's living well.
Some tell me that I expect too much.
That I'm just a man of many dreams.
I dare you to dig through the word.
And find evidence of why I expect all of these many things.
I expect to be filled with gudness!
Given all of God's heavenly means.
From the spiritual unto the physical;
It may take some time to cultivate all of these spiritual things:
I'm expecting peace to God's families;
I'm expecting that we all will grow mightily in the faith;
I'm expecting that Jesus will return,
And remove those that have been given unto him
From this wicked place.
I'm expecting for God to perform miracles .
Small, and or large alltogether!
I'm expecting for God to keep me warm
Through what may seem to be the coldest of all types of weather.
I'm expecting for God to speak through me
In a language that many languages will understand.
I'm expecting for God's angels to fight!
In this and His spiritual land;
With over 10,000 angels on call,
Ready to move with God's hand!
Ask me the reason for this great expectancy,
This hope that I have

Ask Paul the reason for his belief,
Or Peter why he has the faith that he has.
All these things I'm believing, and expecting even more!
Because Jesus is the reason,
And back to the Father he has soared.
My Father shows no partiality!
The same he did through David.
He will do through you and me!
It all comes down to our level of expectancy,
And our amount of belief.

2,000 Years Later 12-18-2011

"The spirirt of the lord God is upon me, because the lord has
anointed me to preach good tidings to the poor; He has sent me
to heal the broken hearted, to proclaim liberty to the captives, and
the opening of the prison to those who are bound; To proclaim the
acceptable year of the lord."

Isaiah 61: 1-2

Has the spirit ever informed you to proclaim something?
That you knew would not come to be today.
Asking yourself are you crazy!
Knowing that this thing could be so far away.
A thousand years as won day,
Or one day to be a thousand years!
With the simple blinking of an eye
This whole lifetime can disappear.
Speak those things that be not
As if they already were.
How do you think Isaiah felt?
When he heard his mouth speaking these foreign words!
And to add insult to injury!
At the day of his death
People just believed he was absurd!
Who would of knew
That the manifestation wouldn't come true?
To 2,000 years after he'd heard.
This is in no way is an attempt to discourage you.
Just to tell you that God does all according to His own
Planning!

"Today this scripture is fulfilled in your hearing."

Luke 9:21

266

Thank You God For Putting Me Up 12-19-2011

Humble me in your goodness,
Exalted and put away.
Many see the worst as bad situations
When God simply has us stored away.
Placed away for your own gudness,
Consecrated from the world.
Lifted up in this high place,
Yet persecuted by the ways of this world.
If I lived my life by the worldly standards;
Then my heavenly standards would fail away.
The things that Jesus has done in this life
Have been done by no other on the way.
My question to be why not!
When his word says that we can do even more.
Either my God is lying,
Or man's faith needs to be elevated unto a whole new floor.
Taken to an all new level
Of moving against the grain.
Not to weigh our status by wealth,
Or how much fame we can claim.
Solomon asked for understanding,
And by wisdom riches came.
We've got this thing all backwards
To the point that we've even removed The King's name.
Thank you for allowing me to see your glory.
Leaving me blinded by the sight of man.
For a time Saul couldn't see in the worldly,
But in time, his sight was reclaimed.

Glory be to God 12-19-2011

When the disciples only wanted to send the people away.
Jesus did the unconventional,
And told them all to sit and stay.
Taking a 5 year olds lunch,
And feeding over 5,000 in a single day.
When common sense
Seems to make no sense
We must turn the mindset to the heavenly way.
Leaning not unto thine own understanding;
Take gifts lowly to the Kings gate.
Even in the times that there seems to be no earthly way.
God has a supernatural way of making a way
Glory, honor and praise to our high God.
And even in the darkness of night,
He will throw down to us tender mercies
And heartfelt blessings.
So how could we ever be crushed by this fate?
I know that the Holy Spirit lives deep within me.
She is great protection;
All that we need.
A forcefield from our enemies.
All the glory be to Christ who holds all might!
All glory and honor be to the King!
Where is it that we would be?
Had you not decided to rest your spirit
Upon us,
Mortal human beings!

Praise God before the Manifestation 12-19-2011

You want to confuse satan?
Then stand up, shout, and clap your hands unto the Lord.
If you want to bring shame on the devil,
Then right now begin to sing and dance unto the Lord.
When we praise God before we can physically see
The manifestation of our unanswered prayers!
satan is confused to no end.
When we praise God in the midst of all worldly confusion
What more is it that he can do but turn and flee!
Knowing that God's word shall come to pass.
No matter how long it may take to come to be.
It's time to mature as God's servants.
I don't want to taunt you;
satan come on home with me!
It's never too late to come back home.
How much would I love to be the one to tell God
The war is One!
The lost son has come home, here to be with us.
The son of perdition is now done.
Praise the Lord for God's goodness
Only Jesus knows the way.
Praise Him for the manifestation,
Though we may never live to See the new day.
Praise God for the manifestation,
Knowing that it's on the way.

Out of the System. 12-19-2011

The King born in swaddling cloth,
Locked out of the inn.
Moses was born poor,
Went prestigeous,
Then went normal again.
The Egyptians were God's people!
Traveling from the way of the world.
Joseph was sold into slavery,
And locked away from the world.
Our God does amazing work
In an irregular way.
From Jews to the Gentiles
God's work .
In His own way.
Jesus was persecuted by the church
Banned out of the synagoggue,
So he sat outside with the blind.
The man he had saved
Ready to perform miracles,
But first by himself he went to go pray.
Even in death,
My Jesus was out of the system.
Being hung on his cross outside of the gates.
Never to be afraid.
To go against the grain.
God will do amazing things,
but only in His own way.

My Tears On This Paper 12-20-2011

Have you ever made a decision?
A mistake that turned out dear to lives?
One move to turn so many peoples world upside down.
When so much of life was going so right.
Here's some for my ex-wife; Apologies I'll always have.
Here's some for those that got hurt that night.
In my prayers a place for you I'll always have.
Here's gallons for my daughters'
You'll always be my heart.
A few more for John and Diane
Thank you for not having a change of heart.
A couple for the Indiana State Police:
Thank you for training me.
More for my family;
Thanks for still believing in me.
Many left for the ripples
That I still do not yet know.
Some left for the ripples,
That still have not yet shown.
Tons of tears for my God!
In whom I love.
Thank you for accepting my repentance for my sins
And giving me a big hug.

I'm Still Gone Praise God 12-21-2011

Though my clothes are all soaked,
And this water so deeply flows.
My shoes aint waterproof,
And I'm soaked all the way up to my throat!
Though the rain keeps on coming,
And I have no rain coat on.
Though the mountains are so high,
And these grey clouds block out all of the sun.
With twenty years down and on my second flop.
With commensary gone low; No more popcorn to pop.
Blood pressure on high, and sugar gone low!
Family member just died,
And to the furneral I can't even go!
Lost as to how to pay the bills!
Unemployment just ran out.
Michigan economics is ranked number 50!
Out of 52 spots.
Heat just got turned off
Unrest all around the world.
Troops on the way home,
But no jobs for them when they return.
The real war is here!
Maybe better to simply stay away.
When you get home, the government has plans to cut your pay.
You may find this letter depressing, but I find it uplifting.
Paul wrote this same kind of letter
While he was locked away
Doing his sentence.

"My brethern, count it all joy when you fall into various trials, knowing that the testing of your faith produces patience, but let patience have it's perfect work, that you may be perfect and complete, lacking nothing."

James 1:2-3

Have You Ever Repented? 12-23-2011

When did you last repent?
All pride to the side.
Tears streaming down your face,
Knees rooted into the ground;
Arms up on high!
Eyes closed; Voice onto the Lord.
Raining down all over you,
When it wasn't even raining before!
The angels in heaven celebrating.
Getting ready to prepare you a way.
God in heaven looking down.
With a big ole smile across His face.
Behind you is satan; Cowering away!
Afraid of the current goodness,
And knowing what is to come to pass at any given day.
Seeing the look in your face,
And hoping that this wont last!
Have you ever repented?
Given to God all that you have.
Saul repented to the world,
And nothing else seemed to work out.
Have you ever repented?
On a direct line by faith!
David called him up with his heart,
And all he did was put the past in its place!
Turned around and God gave back
Everything that he previously had.
Is your pride stopping you?
Or is it time for you to repent?

Ward Of The State 12-24-2011

They say that I'm a ward of the state!
Well what exactly does this mean?
All of my meals to be provided for
Clothing and accessories allotted for me.
Spending monies granted, which I do not have
You go ahead and hold onto that for me.
I'll continue to work hard to collect your tax.
Be it school or work;
Can't make my own outside funds,
Or you threaten to take them away.
From you my power of attorney
I had taken away.
You unwillingly have my body,
But the resources have been given away.
Oversentenced to the maximum,
And held against my will.
Yeah I played a part,
But you know who it was that did this.
Just another way to place me under the ward of you.
Similar to the way you take kids from trying homes
What more Am I to do?
When I've been beaten down to the floor:
Bring wealth into the communities,
If you're really wanting to help us change;
Create some jobs in the hood to help us sustain;
Bring in a clean up crew to help jumpstart,
Separate but equal is our lease on education;
Yeah you can come here if you pay for it.
Once you jump all of those hurdles to make it into this space.
So many have made huge mistakes,
And by skin color they've gone away.
Even though much of it was done on purpose
The state still counted it as a mistake!

Now one bad decision, and look what it has brought onto me!
A ward of the state!
How funny is that to me!

That is happiness; to be dissolved into something complete and
great

Willa Cather

With water all over the place
What makes the flame still burn?
Simply growing higher and higher
In the midst of all the covering dirt!
Fire extinguisher!
Salt!
You just can't stop this burn.
Not even to speak on the logs.
What creates this kind of love?
From whence does such a strong energy cum?
Speak to Moses about the burning bush
See if he can tell you from whence did this fuel exist.
Burning through something consumable
Yet never being consumed by it.
How can something like this be?
It goes against all of the worldly ways;
Fire represents purification,
Up in the hevenly place.
Un-dying to be our loyalty
Such a love one can't ever find.
Put your coins away.
This is something that money cannot buy.

The Heart Of The Woman 12-26-2011

You see the outer,
But inner beauty is what is real.
Encaptured by what she looks like,
When it's what's on the inside
That determines the real.
What's a beautiful smile, and bodacious body?
To an evil heart.
What's the help of plastic surgery,
And even a facelift
If the personality does not play the part.
Tummy tucks and vaginal clips
When the mind is not on par.
Brazilian butt lifts, and chest implants
With sanity lost at heart.
What do we define to be true beauty,
And how do we know when it is lost?
Not found on the cover of Cosmo magazine
Even TV has the wrong people playing the part.
With the world so confused
What is it that my young women are to do next?
Look to the mirror to set your own standards to beauty
Making sure that the heart passes the test.

In The Midst of My Trouble 12-26-2011

I'm sorry that it had to be like this!
You loving me.
Everyday pouring your heart out
While I'm locked up in the penitentiary!
Knowing this was a possibility
I wanted to just push you away.
Your love was simply magnificent!
No way I would let you get away.
If you love something let it go;
Then find me locked away!
If it comes back it's yours to keep;
Thank God I'll be home one day!
Smothered in your love
Never wanting you to get away.
Trapped in our greatness,
Here I will always remain.
Matching the love you've given to me.
Surpassing day by day.
The control center wanting to put limits on our love,
But thank God there is simply no other way.
1 Corinthians 13 to be the decree that we live by!
Looking up this hill, This time away is long!
But looking back it seems to fly bye.
Thank you for undying love, your loyalty and faith.
We've had this conversation before
Never knowing that it would come to be some day!
You will always be the queen of my heart,
And the priestess of my faith.
Time apart can be a painful thing, to live through for lovers,
But we will make it day by day.
Standing here heart to heart,
And faith to faith.

Moving Forward In The Lord 12-27-2011

Just made it one more step today!
A step that I never thought I could take.
Done journeyed for many miles now
Still thinking back to that first stake;
That I couldn't believe that I could take.
Moving forward inch by inch,
Even when it feels stagnant in my mind.
What do I do to keep the mind off of this?
And the focus heavily placed upon Christ!
I used to ask God to save me!
Until I realized that this isn't my life.
Now I know that it's all for God's glory.
Whatever he decides to do with this life!
I'm giving up all resistance!
Praying for the Holy Spirit to guide my mind.
I Am but a vessel.
A cistern honored to hold Her life!
Thank you for allotting me resources,
And giving me the heart to pour this back unto the world.
You are the only reason I keep believing.
Knowing that you will bring me back to my girls.

"And certain women who had been healed of evil spirits and infirmities. Mary called Magdalene, out of whom had come seven demons, and Joanna the wife of Chuza, Herod's steward, and Susanna, and many others who provided for him from their substance.

Luke 8:2-3

No disrecpect to Ruth and Esther,
But I'm on the hunt for more.
The samaratan woman!
Where have all of the Mary's gone?
Women not to be teachers;
A tradition of the times.
Well without that woman!
What would have happened to the spies?
What's the results of the story of Anna the widow?
Who for over 80 years faithfully prayed?
What ever happened to the poor widow?
Who out of her poverty gave?
To look you up in the concordance.
Your reference is everywhere,
But when I search for you in the table of contents
I'm finding you no-where.
From A woman caught up in adultry,
To a woman of great faith.
Jesus needing these women to illustrate his story,
Yet they headline in no place.
What's the testamony of Simon's mother,
Who Jesus raised?
The sinful woman with the alabaster jar of perfume;
You wet Jesus feet with your tears!
And dried them with your hair!
I need to know,
What happened to you in accordance to your faith.
You only touched his hem,

And the 18 year flow of blood was stopped
Your faith healed you, and peace is what you got.
What made you so brave?
And through your fear so bold?
Another piece of useful information,
That I would just love to know.
Who are Joanna and Susanna? Presented in chapter 8.
If these were the original twelve disciples?
Then why are their proclamations the ones locked away?
Would I be asking too much?
For a first hand account of what happend at the tomb?
I know that at least one of these women
Kept account of the news,
But what we learn is of knowledge that's already been used.
Did Miriam have a song book?
Of exodus 15:21?
Deborah sat under the palm tree
Giving out wisdom in judgement for the children
In need of a judge.
Where is the chapter on Huldah?
Because like Moses, She spoke saying, "Thus says the Lord"
Isaiah's is one of the biggest books of the bible
So why only in verse eight line three
Do we hear the prophetess speak?
The daughters of Phillip,
Located in Acts 21: 8 through 9.
The word says thay you prophesied
So where can your prophetesses be?

The older women likewise, that they be reverent in behavior, not
slanderers, not given to much wine, teachers of good things-
Titus 2:3

The Change That I See 12-31-2011

"They will perish, but you will endure; Yes, they will all grow old like a garment; Like a cloak you will change them, and they will be changed. But you are the same , and your years will have no end.
Psalm 102:26,27

There's a balance to our planet., The pulse that keeps it alive.
So many things that we take for granted,
But what happens if this planet was to die?
2/3's of the polar bears have gone extinct
Since 1965!
Glaciers starting to disappear,
And ocean levels on the rise!
Wolverines dwindle in numbers.
So many other animals too!
Oil consumption on the rise,
And spills keep happening like nothing new.

Global warming to plate techtonics,
Who is there that could change that?
Still confused?
Then I suggest you turn to Psalm 103 verses 26 and 27
And take a read through that.

Malachi is the end, but of the new beginning he proclaims.
Take just a quick second to read chapter 6, verse three again.

From finances to people, all of this must come to change.
Moving from bartering, to schillings, to currency
And now with debits cards we financially trade.

Uncommon sicknesses! Incurable STD's.
Animals and livestock becoming sick,
And then we eat the meat.

So much disappearance,
Of what grew abundantly once before;
Cutting down all of God's trees
So for capitalism we can create more.
Look at us trampling through God's garden
Acting like we know the correct way.
From space stations to missles
Just wanting to find, conqure, and blow up some empty space!
My God's word never lies.
And it says he will be coming back some day.

If we know Job to be a wise man,
Then turn to 23:13!
Although all of this must fade away,
We will still lean on the king.

"I Am the Lord, I do not change; Therefore you are not
consumed, O sons of Jacob."

Malachi 3:6

Touch This Situation 12-31-2011

"Then they willingly received him into the boat, and
immediately the boat was at the land where they were going."
John 6:21

The disciples paddled hard, and just could not seem to get there.
Along you came to touch the situation,
And miraculously they were landed right there.
Show me how to willingly receive you!
By Mark 5:36 show me how not to be afraid;
Only to believe. Knowing we headed in the right way.
Lord the rent is past due,
And the refrigerator holds not much to eat.
Psalm 35:27 says that you delight in the prosperity of those you
Lead.
Well what is the matter with me?
This Michigan winter has been oh so cold,
And this apartment holds no heat.
Kidney stones are once again bothering my soul;
Please God help them to pass away
According to Isaiah, 53: 3 and 4.
Pain cannot successfully live in this frame.
If that be true, then why so often does this tent ache?
Small discrepencies in the church,
Seeming to manifest day by day.
satan you have no home in this residence.
According to James 4 and 7, I cast you far away.
I command the angels to bless this situation.
In compliance to Psalm 103 and verse 20.
My kids hearts are beginning to turn cold,
And even they are beginning to mock at me.
Why do I have such faith?
What's the reason for this complete surrender to you that I have.
As John 8:50, allow this to be all for God's behalf;
His hand touching this situation that I have.

"So shall my word be that goes forth from my mouth; It shall not return to me void. But it shall accomplish what I please, and it shall prosper in the thing for which I sent it."

Isaiah 55:11

Remember that not getting what you want is sometimes a wonderful stroke of luck.

Dalai Lama

Also available by Jones Publishing LLC

No Fear: The Lords Redemption
By Elton Jones

Quarantine: To Break Free
By Elton Jones

ABC Poetry
By Katy Rios

Next to come by Jones Publishing

2012
2013
2014
2015
2016
Exposed